Ready to take your journey to the next level?

Your purchase of "Reclaim Sobriety: 12 Rounds to Sobriety" is just the beginning. As a special gift to our dedicated Gladiators, we're offering you FREE lifetime access to the Reclaim Sobriety On-Demand BootCamp. This exclusive 8-session course is designed to complement your reading, allowing you to dive deeper into the strategies and worksheets at your own pace. Let Ken guide you personally through each exercise, helping you unlock your full potential and solidify your path to lasting sobriety. Don't miss this opportunity to supercharge your recovery journey.

Simply visit reclaimsobriety.com/gift to claim your free access today. Remember, true warriors never stop training – your next level of strength and resilience awaits! go to https://reclaimsobriety.com or scan the QR code.

Reclaim Sobriety

12 Rounds of Sobriety

Contents

The Weigh-In

(OR HOW TO SIZE UP YOUR OPPONENT AND GET READY FOR THE FIGHT OF YOUR LIFE)

ALRIGHT, FUTURE GLADIATORS. BEFORE we step into the ring for our 12 rounds of sobriety, we need to weigh in. This isn't just some bullshit formality. This is where we take a hard look at ourselves, size up our opponent (that bastard called addiction), and get our heads in the game for the fight ahead.

Now, let me tell you something about weighing in. It's not always pretty. Sometimes, you've got to strip down, stand under those harsh lights, and face some ugly truths. But that's exactly what we're going to do here. Because if you can't be honest with yourself now, you don't stand a chance in the ring.

Let me share my weigh-in moment with you. It wasn't my first rodeo, mind you. I'd been drinking heavily my whole life. I tried to quit a couple of times when I got in trouble like when I was 13; you will learn more about that later. I'd successfully quit drinking for a while, but I was always playing that moderation game. You know the one, right? "I can handle just one drink." Spoiler alert: We can't.

For years, I was living what looked like the dream. Operating data centers since I was 24. The infrastructure, the 24/7 hustle, competing against some of the world's largest companies - I loved it. It was in my blood. But let me tell you, that lifestyle can be a bitch when you're wrestling with a booze problem.

2016 was a particularly hard year. I'd just been promoted from vice president to president of the company I helped found. Sounds great, right? Except my co-founder, Steve, was leaving because of throat cancer. And that was just the start of the shit storm.

Now, I've been through some tough times before: near-fatal car accidents (plural) and multiple arrests. Hell, when I was 20, I got hit by an 18-wheeler going 80 miles per hour and spent 18 months in physical rehab. I dislocated both shoulders, blew out discs in my back, hyperextended my neck, and had brain stem swelling. The works. But this? This was one of the hardest moments of my life.

My largest shareholder gave me the chance to figure things out without my predecessor right in the middle of one of the most challenging economic times we'd ever seen. Our largest client, one of the biggest coal manufacturers in the country, had just gone bankrupt and discontinued our services. That was a huge chunk of our revenue gone. And that was just one of a dozen issues weighing on me.

Now, I can't tell you if I was drinking more or less during this time. As far back as I can remember, probably since my early twenties, I was averaging 6 to 20 beers a day. And that was just the appetizer. The main course was at least a pint of whiskey, often a fifth or more. In my younger days, it probably would've been vodka. I had a soft spot for vodka and lemonade.

But here's where it all came to a head. One night, we had a problem at one of our data centers in downtown St. Louis. Downtown St. Louis at 2 AM isn't exactly Disneyland if you know what I mean. But I had to go. I had strep throat that week, so I hadn't been drinking. Not because I was trying to quit, mind you. I just felt like shit.

So there I was, fixing whatever was broken in the middle of the night. Everyone else had left, and I was wrapping up a call, thinking I might hit the bar for a couple of beers before heading home. (Side note: 24/7 bars? Beautiful place for an alcoholic. Terrible place for someone trying to get sober.)

I walked into our heat mitigation room - imagine a 10,000-square-foot warehouse running at about 90 to 100°F. Suddenly, I was dizzy as hell. I lay down on the floor, my heart's going crazy; I didn't know where I was. I thought I was going to die.

It turned out it was a panic attack. It was not my first, but it was different from any other. I ended up in the ER and then at my doctor's office the next day. They were running tests and asking questions. "Do you still drink?" they asked. "Yes," I said, because, in my mind, I did.

Then the doctor asked, "When was your last drink?" And it was like a light bulb went off over his head. "Oh," he said, "you're going through withdrawals."

Now, this doctor was a good old boy. He looked at me, concern all over his face, and said something I'll never forget: "If you keep drinking, you might have two years of life left. But luckily for you, your liver's not all the way gone yet. You can have a full recovery if you want to quit drinking now. I'll help you if you want. If not, go home and keep drinking. All these symptoms will probably go away quickly as soon as you have a beer. But you'll be done in a couple of years."

That, my friends, was my weigh-in moment. That was when I had to strip down, metaphorically speaking, and took a good, hard look at myself. And let me tell you, I didn't like what I saw.

Now, I'd love to tell you that I quit right then and there, rode off into the sunset, and lived happily ever after. But that's not how this shit works.

I took his advice reluctantly. I didn't want to quit. That led to a couple of years of Xanax addiction, which I don't recommend to anyone. The withdrawals from Xanax? They're a special kind of hell.

I played the moderation game for a while after that. I even convinced that same doctor later on that I could handle a drink here and there. Spoiler alert: I couldn't.

So, if there's anybody out there who thinks this is an easy road or that you can just drink non-alcoholic beer and call it a day, you're in for a rude awakening. This game we're playing? It's fucking hard. It's going to take everything you've got. You're going to exercise every mental muscle you have, and you're going to find things about yourself that you never knew existed.

But I promise you this: You can navigate your way through this shit and find your way to sobriety. When you do, it'll feel like a million weights have been lifted off your chest. All the chains will be broken from your wrists, ankles, and waist. The coffin will be opened, and you can walk out and live a happy, authentic life.

That's what these 12 rounds of sobriety are all about. Whether you're just starting out or you've quit before but struggle with relapses and cravings, we will tackle this thing head-on. We're going to redefine who we are. Because, let's face it, being an addict? It's fucking pathetic, and it's not something any of us want to be.

So here are what we're going to do in these 12 rounds:

1. We're going to face our shit. No more excuses, no more bullshit.

2. We're going to learn some tools and strategies to fight this bastard called addiction.

3. We're going to change how we see ourselves. We're not victims;

we're not "recovering addicts." We're Sobriety Gladiators.

4. We're going to build a life so fucking awesome that alcohol looks like the weak sauce it really is.

This isn't going to be easy. There will be days when you want to throw in the towel. Days when you think you can't do it. But remember this: If one flawed, fucked-up human like me can do it, so can you.

So, are you ready to step on the scale? Are you ready to face your opponent? Are you ready to become a Sobriety Gladiator?

Let's do this. The fight of your life is about to begin.

Round 1: Embracing Control

(OR HOW TO STOP BEING ADDICTION'S BITCH AND BECOME A SOBRIETY GLADIATOR)

WELCOME TO THE ARENA, Gladiators. You're here because you're ready to fight the battle of your life – the battle for your sobriety. This isn't just about putting down the bottle. It's about transforming your entire fucking mindset. It's about shedding that weak, powerless addict skin and emerging as a warrior in control of your own destiny.

Now, I know some of you might be coming from AA, and you're probably thinking, "But wait, I thought I was supposed to admit I'm powerless?" Well, buckle up, buttercup, because we're about to flip that script.

The Addiction Mindset vs. The Sober Mindset

Let's get one thing straight: Having an addiction mindset and admitting you're powerless might be a good starting point, but they're not the tools you need for long-term recovery. They're like training wheels – useful when just starting, but if you keep them on, you'll never learn to really ride the bike.

Here's the hard truth: Identifying as an alcoholic is no way to live. It's a self-fulfilling prophecy that keeps you trapped in a cycle of shame and relapse. Instead, we're going to identify as sober men and women. We will choose the kind of person we want to be because we become whatever we tell ourselves we are.

Think about it. When you say, "I'm an alcoholic," what image does that conjure up? Probably someone weak, out of control, always one drink away from disaster. But when you say, "I'm a sober warrior," or "I'm a Sobriety Gladiator," that paints a whole different picture. Strength. Control. Power. That's the mindset we're cultivating here.

The Power of Identity

I grew up in a house where criminal activity was the norm. There's a quote that says, "A child living in a house of thieves will find guilt in the fact that he himself is not a thief." This speaks volumes about the importance of identifying your ideal self.

Throughout life, one thing that's bound to make you suffer is when your actions conflict with your core values. So, our first task as Sobriety Gladiators is to establish our core values. We will repeat these values every day until they become part of who we are. This is a significant part of always being ready.

But what does this look like in practice? Let's break it down:

1. Identify Your Values: What matters most to you? Is it honesty? Courage? Compassion? Write these down.

2. Define What They Mean to You: For example, if one of your values is integrity, what does that look like in your daily life?

3. Live Them Daily: Look for opportunities to embody the values in your actions, big and small.

    4. Reflect and Adjust: At the end of each day, ask yourself if you lived up to your values. If not, don't beat yourself up. Learn from it and do better tomorrow.

Remember, this isn't about being perfect. It's about striving to be better, to be the person you want to be, every single day.

Always Be Ready: The Gladiator's Mantra

Now, let's talk about this "Always Be Ready" mindset. This isn't just some cute slogan. It's a way of life. It's about being prepared for every trigger, craving, and moment of weakness before it happens.

Let me tell you a story. I was in Florida for a summit to see Mr. Beast. I'd been sober for about four years at this point, with only a handful of relapses. I walked into a local pizza joint because I had a couple of hours to kill between speakers. One of my old excuses for drinking used to be if they didn't have Diet Coke with my food, I'd go for a beer or get Diet Pepsi with a couple of shots of Crown Royal.

That day, they only had Pepsi. Instinctually, I ordered a beer. And instantly, I knew it was a mistake. Why? Because I'd done the work. I'd established my core values. I'd trained myself to be ready. That gut feeling of wrongness? That's what being ready feels like.

Contrast that with the people I talk to every week who relapse. Every one of them tells me how guilty they feel after the fact. They didn't have the tools. They didn't do the work to always be ready for the triggers.

So, how do we cultivate this "Always Be Ready" mindset? Here are some strategies:

    1. Know Your Triggers: Identify the people, places, situations, and emotions that make you want to drink.

2. Plan Ahead: For each trigger, have a specific plan of action. What will you do instead of drinking?

3. Practice Mindfulness: Stay aware of your thoughts and feelings. The more aware you are, the less likely you are to react on autopilot.

4. Visualize Success: Regularly imagine yourself successfully navigating triggering situations without drinking.

5. Build a Support Network: Have people you can call when struggling. Ensure they know they're part of your "Always Be Ready" strategy.

6. Keep Your Why Front and Center: Regularly remind yourself why you chose sobriety. Make it visceral and emotional.

The Importance of Preparation

Let me give you another example from my boxing days. I had a young fighter, 13 or 14 years old, showing up for his very first match. We'd gone through everything to make him ready for this fight. He was fully dressed, we'd practiced footwork, and everything seemed good to go.

But when I asked him if he was comfortable, he mentioned his cup was really uncomfortable. It turns out that this kid had his athletic cup upside down. He'd never worn it in practice, so he didn't know how to do his footwork with that extra business between his legs.

We got all the way to fight night, no more than 45 minutes away from stepping into the ring for the first time, and this crucial detail was overlooked. The point is, he wasn't ready. And quite honestly, I failed him as a coach.

This is a testament that when you're ready, and you've done all the work when that opportunity hits you, that trigger hits you, that craving hits you, something as silly as not knowing how to put your cup on right can be the determining factor in that fight.

In recovery, your "cup" might be knowing how to handle a social situation without drinking or how to manage stress without turning to alcohol. You need to practice these skills before you're in the heat of the moment.

Building Your Gladiator Arsenal

So, how do we make sure we're always ready? Here's your Gladiator arsenal:

1. Core Values: Establish them, repeat them daily, and live by them. They're your shield against temptation.

2. Exit Strategies: Know your triggers and have a plan for each one. If certain places, people, or situations are dangerous for your sobriety, have a way out planned.

3. Mindfulness: Stay present. 100% of my relapses happened when I wasn't thinking at all. I was just reacting. I was letting life happen to me instead of owning it and being the Gladiator I know I am.

4. Self-Love: Look in the mirror daily and tell yourself, "I love and respect you." It might feel cheesy at first but do it anyway. You need to be your own biggest supporter in this fight.

5. Positive Identity: Stop identifying as an addict or alcoholic. You're a sober warrior now. Own it.

Let's dive deeper into each of these:

Core Values: Your core values are your personal constitution. They guide your decisions and actions. When you're faced with a choice, ask yourself, "Does this align with my values?" If not, it's probably not the right choice for you.

Exit Strategies: An exit strategy isn't about running away. It's about being smart and protecting your sobriety. Maybe it's having a trusted friend you can call to pick you up from a triggering situation. Perhaps it's always driving yourself so you can leave when necessary. Whatever it is, have it planned out in advance.

Mindfulness: Mindfulness is about being aware of your thoughts, feelings, and surroundings in the present moment. It's a powerful tool against the autopilot behavior that often leads to relapse. Start with just a few minutes of mindfulness practice each day. Focus on your breath, notice your thoughts without judging them, and bring your attention back to the present moment whenever it wanders.

Self-Love: This one's tough for a lot of us. We've spent years beating ourselves up, feeling shame and guilt. But self-love is crucial to recovery. Start small. Find one thing you like about yourself each day. Treat yourself with the same kindness you'd show a good friend. Remember, you're worth fighting for.

Positive Identity: The language we use to describe ourselves is powerful. When you say, "I am a sober warrior" instead of "I am an alcoholic," you're not just changing words. You're changing your entire self-concept. You're telling your brain, "This is who I am now." And your brain will work to make that true.

The Gladiator's Mindset

Now, I want to address something that might be a mind-fuck for some of you. We're going to embrace control. That's right. None of this "let go and let God" bullshit. You are in control of your destiny.

I don't want to knock AA too much. It's done a lot of good for a lot of people. But the idea that you're not in control of your destiny? That's grade-A bullshit. Once you get past the acute withdrawal syndrome and you're dealing with the real work of recovery, having those built-in excuses of powerlessness is a surefire way to end up right back at the bottle.

You are not powerless. You are a fucking Gladiator. You have the power to choose, to fight, and to win—every single day.

This mindset shift is crucial. When you believe you're powerless, you're already defeated. But when you embrace control, you're empowered. You're no longer a victim of your addiction. You're a warrior fighting for your life and your future.

Here's how to cultivate the Gladiator mindset:

1. Take Responsibility: Your choices got you here, and your choices will get you out. Own that.

2. Embrace Challenges: Every craving, every trigger, every difficult situation is an opportunity to grow stronger.

3. Learn from Setbacks: Don't wallow in guilt if you slip up. Analyze what happened and use that knowledge to do better next time.

4. Celebrate Victories: Every day sober is a win. Acknowledge your progress, no matter how small it might seem.

5. Keep Growing: A Gladiator never stops training. Always be learning, always be improving.

The Daily Battle

Here's the thing about being a Sobriety Gladiator: the fight never ends. You don't get to hang up your sword and retire. But that's okay because each day you stay sober, you get stronger. Each craving you overcome, each trigger you navigate, each day you choose your sober life over your old drinking life, you're winning.

Your job is to wake up every day and choose to be a Gladiator. Choose to be ready. Choose to be in control. It's not easy. There will be days when you want to throw in the towel and days when the old addiction mindset tries to creep back in. But that's why we're here. That's why we're Gladiators.

Remember: You can't always be 100% ready because you can only be as ready as where you are right now. And that's okay. Start using the tools. Start doing the work. Use the worksheets at the back of this book. We will go over all kinds of tips and tricks to help you stay ready, stay in control, and stay mindful.

Here's what your daily battle might look like:

Morning:

- Wake up and immediately reaffirm your identity: "I am a Sobriety Gladiator."

- Review your core values.

- Practice mindfulness or meditation.

- Plan your day, including strategies for any potential triggers.

Throughout the Day:

- Stay mindful. Check in with yourself regularly.

- Use positive self-talk to reinforce your Gladiator identity.

- When faced with challenges, ask yourself, "What would a Sobriety Gladiator do?"

Evening:

- Reflect on your day. What went well? What could you improve?

- Practice gratitude. What are you thankful for in your sober life?

- Plan for tomorrow.

Night:

- Engage in a relaxing, sober bedtime routine.

- Visualize yourself succeeding as a Sobriety Gladiator.

Your Gladiator Homework

1. Write out your core values. What principles do you want to live by in your sober life?

2. Identify your top 5 triggers and create an exit strategy for each one.

3. Start a daily mindfulness practice. Even 5 minutes a day can make a huge difference.

4. Begin each day by looking in the mirror and saying, "I love and respect you." End each day by acknowledging one way you acted like a Sobriety Gladiator.

5. Write out your new identity statement. "I am [Your Name], and I am a Sobriety Gladiator." Repeat it to yourself daily.

6. Create a vision board of your ideal sober life. Include images and

words that represent who you want to be and what you want to achieve.

7. Start a Gladiator Journal. Use it to track your progress, work through challenges, and celebrate victories.

Conclusion: Stepping into the Arena

You're not just here to stop drinking. You're here to transform your entire fucking life. You're here to become a warrior, a Gladiator in the arena of sobriety.

Remember, this journey isn't about perfection. It's about progress. It's about showing up every day, ready to fight. It's about taking control of your life, one decision at a time.

You've taken the first step by picking up this book. Now, it's time to step into the arena and start throwing punches. Your opponent is tough, but guess what? You're tougher.

You have the power to rewrite your story. You have the strength to overcome your addiction. You have the courage to face life on life's terms without numbing yourself.

From this moment on, you're not a victim. You're not powerless. You're a Sobriety Gladiator. You're a warrior in the most important battle of your life.

So, are you ready to embrace control and start this journey? Are you ready to become the badass, sober Gladiator you never knew existed? The choice is yours, warrior. Now, let's get ready for Round 2.

Remember: In the arena of life, it's not about how hard you can hit. It's about how hard you can get hit and keep moving forward. That's how winning is done. That's how Sobriety Gladiators are made.

Now go out there and show addiction who's boss. You've got this, Gladiator.

Round 2: Building Strength

(OR HOW TO STOP BEING A WET NOODLE IN RECOVERY)

ALRIGHT, GLADIATORS. WELCOME BACK to the arena. You've survived Round 1, but don't get cocky. We're about to dive deep into some real shit here. We're talking about building the kind of strength that doesn't just keep you sober but turns you from a rage-fueled, flip-off-everyone-on-the-highway maniac into someone who can actually enjoy this clusterfuck we call life.

The Core Value That'll Save Your Ass

Let's start with a core value that's going to change your fucking life: Treat Every Person You Interact With, Like You Would Like Them to Treat You.

Now, I know what you're thinking. "Isn't that just the Golden Rule? Did I get sober just to end up in Sunday School?" Hold your horses, smartass. This isn't your grandma's life advice. This is the kind of wisdom that comes from years of fucking up and finally getting your shit together.

The Passionate Man's Dilemma

Let me tell you something about myself: I'm a passionate man. And during my active addiction, and even post-withdrawal, that passion often translated into being a complete and utter asshole.

Picture this: I, driving down the highway, flipping people off left and right because they dared to drive too slow or swerve a little in their lane. Hell, there were times I chased people down, trying to get them out of their cars to fight me on the side of the road. All because I was so goddamn angry and not practicing this core value.

Sound familiar? Maybe you haven't gone full road rage warrior, but I bet you've had moments where your emotions took the wheel and drove you straight into Asshole Town.

The Wake-Up Call

Here's the kicker: I originally created these core values for my students. Yeah, Mr. Wise Guy here thought he had it all figured out. But when I did some real self-reflection, I realized something that hit me like a ton of bricks: These weren't just for my students. These were the tools I needed to overcome this fucking alcoholism that had been running my life.

It took me a long time to figure out what I really wanted in life. And you know what? I think it's what everybody truly wants: To enjoy life free of conflict. I don't want to get in anybody's way, and I don't want anybody to get in my way. I just want to enjoy the beautiful gift of life that I've been given.

Sounds simple, right? But let me tell you, it's anything but easy.

The Transformation

Implementing this core value was like trying to turn a battleship with a paddle. It doesn't happen overnight. But little by little, interaction by interaction, I started to change.

Instead of flipping off the guy who cut me off in traffic, I started to think, "Maybe he's having a shitty day. Maybe he just found out his kid is sick or his wife left him. How would I want to be treated if I was in his shoes?"

It wasn't easy. There were days when I wanted to say, "fuck it" and go back to my old ways. But here's the thing: Every time I treated someone with kindness and respect, even when they didn't "deserve" it, I felt a little bit stronger. A little more in control. A little more like the man I wanted to be.

The Ripple Effect

Here's something wild I discovered: When you start treating people how you want to be treated, it creates a ripple effect. Not only do people often respond kindly, but you start to feel different about yourself.

Think about it. When you treat someone with respect, even when they're being a dick, you're not just changing the dynamic of that interaction. You're changing how you see yourself. You're becoming the kind of person who can rise above petty bullshit. And let me tell you, that kind of self-respect is worth more than all the booze in the world.

The Key to Happiness

Now, let's talk about happiness. Because isn't that what we're all after? We drank to be happy, we got sober to be happy, and now we're doing all this self-improvement shit to be happy.

Well, I've got a little secret for you. It's Bashir's key to happiness: Follow your passion to the greatest of your capabilities as frequently and aggressively as you can with no expectation of the outcome.

Let that sink in for a minute. Follow your passion. Aggressively. But here's the kicker - with no expectation of the outcome.

This ties directly into our core values. When treating others how you want to be treated, you're not doing it because you expect something in return. You're doing it because it's the right thing to do. Because it aligns with your values. Because it makes you the kind of person you want to be.

The Same Goes for Sobriety

Think about how this applies to your sobriety. You're not staying sober because you expect life to suddenly become all rainbows and unicorns. You're doing it because it aligns with who you want to be. Because it allows you to follow your passions and to live life fully and authentically.

And let me tell you, when you approach sobriety this way - passionately, aggressively, but without attachment to outcomes - that's when the magic happens. That's when you start to find real, lasting happiness.

Practical Steps to Implement This Core Value

Alright, enough philosophy. Let's get down to the nitty-gritty. How do you actually put this shit into practice? Here are some steps:

1. Morning Mindset: Start each day by reminding yourself of this core value. Say it out loud: "Today, I will treat every person I interact with like I would like them to treat me."

2. Trigger Identification: Make a list of situations that typically trigger your asshole behavior. Traffic? Work stress? Family drama? Knowing your triggers is half the battle.

3. Pause and Reflect: When you feel yourself about to react negatively, pause. Take a deep breath. Ask yourself, "Is this how I would want to be treated in this situation?"

4. Empathy Exercise: Put yourself in someone else's shoes once a day. The cashier who seems grumpy? The coworker who's being

difficult? Imagine what might be going on in their life.

5. Gratitude Practice: Each night, write down three instances where someone treated you well. This helps you focus on the positive and reminds you of how you want to be treated.

6. Amends and Forgiveness: When you mess up (and you will), make amends quickly. And just as importantly, forgive yourself. Remember, we're aiming for progress, not perfection.

7. Passion Pursuit: Identify what you're passionate about. Make time each day to engage in that passion, even just for a few minutes.

The Challenge of Consistency

Now, I'm not going to bullshit you. Living by this core value consistently is tough as nails. There will be days when you want to tell the world to go fuck itself. Days when being kind and respectful feel as natural as a fish riding a bicycle.

But here's the thing: In those moments, this core value becomes most important. It's easy to be kind when everything's going your way. The real test comes when life is kicking your ass six ways from Sunday.

Remember what we talked about in Round 1? Being a Gladiator isn't about being perfect. It's about getting back up every time you fall. So when you have a day where you fail to live up to this core value, don't beat yourself up. Acknowledge it, learn from it, and commit to doing better tomorrow.

The Power of Vulnerability

Here's something that might make you uncomfortable: Treating others the way you want to be treated often requires vulnerability. It means being honest about your feelings, admitting when you're wrong, and asking for help when you need it.

In our drinking days, we might have seen vulnerability as a weakness. But let me tell you; it takes a hell of a lot more strength to be vulnerable than it does to hide behind a bottle or a tough-guy facade.

When you're vulnerable, you're showing others that you trust them. You're opening yourself up to deeper connections. And in recovery, those connections can be lifelines.

The Compound Effect

The beautiful thing about living by this core value is that it has a compound effect. Each positive interaction, each moment of treating someone well, builds on the last. Over time, it becomes a habit. It becomes who you are.

And as it becomes who you are, your strength grows. Your resilience increases. Your ability to face life's challenges without turning to alcohol gets stronger and stronger.

It's like compound interest for your character. Small, consistent actions, over time, lead to massive growth.

Handling Conflict

Now, let's talk about conflict. Because let's face it, life isn't always sunshine and rainbows. Sometimes people are going to treat you like shit, no matter how well you treat them. So what do you do then?

First, remember that their behavior is about them, not you. You can't control how others act, but you can control your response.

Second, set boundaries. Treating others well doesn't mean being a doormat. You can be kind and respectful while still standing up for yourself.

Third, use conflict as an opportunity for growth. Ask yourself, "What can I learn from this situation? How can I handle this in a way that aligns with my values?"

Your Gladiator Homework

Alright, Gladiators. It's time to put this into action. Here's your homework for the week:

1. Write out the core value: "Treat Every Person You Interact With, Like You Would Like Them to Treat You." Put it somewhere you'll see it every day.

2. Each morning, set an intention for how you want to treat others and be treated that day.

3. Keep a daily log of your interactions—note times when you lived up to this core value and times when you fell short. No judgment, just observation.

4. At the end of each day, reflect on how living by this core value made you feel. Did it make you feel stronger? More in control?

5. Practice one act of vulnerability each day. It could be as simple as admitting you don't know something or asking for help with a task.

6. Identify one relationship in your life where you can start applying this core value more consistently. What specific actions can you take to treat this person the way you'd want to be treated?

7. Spend at least 15 minutes each day pursuing your passion, with no expectation of outcome. Just do it for its sheer joy.

8. At the end of the week, write a letter to yourself about what you've

learned from this exercise. How has it changed your perspective? How has it built your strength?

Conclusion: The Strength of Character

Remember, Gladiators, we're not just building physical strength here. We're not even just staying sober. We're building strength of character. We're forging ourselves into the kind of people who can face life's challenges head-on without needing to numb ourselves with alcohol or lash out in anger.

Treating every person you interact with like you would like them to treat you isn't just about being nice. It's about building a foundation of self-respect, integrity, and resilience that will support you throughout your recovery journey and beyond.

It's about becoming the kind of person who doesn't need to drink to face the world—the kind of person who can look themselves in the mirror and be proud of who they see.

Keep this core value at the forefront of your mind as you move forward. Let it guide your actions, your words, and your thoughts. Let it be the standard by which you measure your growth.

You're becoming a better, stronger version of yourself. You're becoming a true Gladiator. And you're learning to enjoy the beautiful gift of life you've been given.

Now get out there and show the world what you're made of. Round 3 is coming, and it's going to take everything you've got. But you've got this, Gladiator. You're stronger than you know.

Remember: Life is too short for road rage and resentment. Treat others well, pursue your passions, and enjoy the ride. That's what being a Sobriety Gladiator is all about.

Round 3: Mindset Transformation

(OR HOW TO SHOW UP WITH POSITIVITY WHEN LIFE'S KICKING YOUR ASS)

ALRIGHT, GLADIATORS. YOU'VE MADE it through two rounds, and you're still standing. Now it's time for the real fight – the one that happens between your ears. Welcome to Round 3: Mindset Transformation. This is where we dig deep into the shit that's been holding you back and rewire that trauma-soaked brain of yours to show up with positivity, even when life feels like a sucker punch to the gut.

The Core Value: Show Up with Positivity

Let's start with our core value for this round: Show Up with Positivity. Now, I know what you're thinking. "Positivity? In this fucked-up world? While I'm battling addiction? You've got to be shitting me." Trust me, I get it. This isn't about slapping on a fake smile and pretending everything's sunshine and rainbows. It's about rewiring your brain to find the silver lining, even in the stormiest clouds.

The Roots of Our Negativity

Let me tell you a story about yours truly. I grew up in a Section 8 neighborhood, moving from apartments to a house with three stepbrothers and a stepsister. We always had other kids living with us. It was a damn the man environment – bikers, strip clubs, drugs, and alcohol everywhere. An "honor amongst thieves" kind of world where we didn't have much, but we had this twisted sense of community.

This environment didn't exactly breed positivity. It bred survival instincts, distrust, and a "fuck the world before it fucks you" mentality. Men drank beer, got in fights, and showed emotions about as often as a cat takes a bath. Positivity? That was for weak-minded fools who couldn't handle reality.

But let me share another story that really hammers home how these negative beliefs get planted early. I was seven years old and at a party on a Sunday evening. I spotted a fuzzy navel on the table - I didn't know what it was at the time. It just looked like a fucking orange juice to me. Now, it was common for me to get a little tipsy on beer, but I hadn't had any hard liquor yet.

I looked at my mom and said, "Can I have that?" Without flinching, my 27-year-old mother, struggling with her own alcohol issues and trauma, looked at me and said, "If you're man enough, go for it."

Now, I want to be clear - I don't blame her for that decision. I love my mother, and our relationship today is stronger than ever. We've worked through our issues, we understand where we came from, we've forgiven each other, and we're living healthy lives, supporting each other.

But that moment? That was the first time I got drunk on any kind of hard liquor. I didn't know why I could drink so much alcohol, but it became literally a novelty for people and myself to see how much I could drink. That night, I probably had six or seven of those fuzzy navels.

This shit plants deep roots, Gladiators. It shapes your idea of what it means to be a man, to be strong, and to be worthy. And let me tell you, learning to show up with positivity when your foundation is built on this kind of quicksand? It's a fucking challenge.

But here's the thing - if I can do it, so can you. It starts with recognizing these toxic beliefs for what they are - bullshit that was fed to us when we were too young to know better. Once you see it, you can start to change it.

The EMDR Revolution

It took EMDR (Eye Movement Desensitization and Reprocessing) for me to uncover where these negative beliefs came from and how to reframe them. If you haven't heard of EMDR, it's a psychotherapy treatment designed to alleviate the distress associated with traumatic memories. I highly recommend reading "The Body Keeps the Score" – that book taught me about EMDR and changed my fucking life.

Through EMDR, I realized that my negative outlook wasn't just "being realistic." It was a defense mechanism to protect myself from disappointment and pain. But here's the kicker – it was also keeping me stuck in a cycle of addiction and misery.

The Vulnerability of Positivity

Here's another mind-fuck I had to overcome: Showing up with positivity requires vulnerability. In my world, vulnerability was for pussies. "Why you being a little bitch? Suck it up, pussy." These phrases were the soundtrack of my youth, and I had no tools to defend myself against these accusations.

So what did I do? I armored up with alcohol. I started drinking heavier at the age of 10, but I'd been stealing sips of beer since I was three. Hell, I missed my first day of school because I was too drunk at the age of seven. Alcohol was my way of numbing the pain, of avoiding vulnerability, of pretending everything was fine when it was anything but.

Redefining Strength

Through my recovery journey, I've had to completely redefine what it means to be strong. Being strong isn't about how much you can drink or how tough you are in a fight. It's about having the courage to show up with positivity even when life is kicking your ass. It's about being able to look challenging things in the face, move forward through the hard shit without the crutch of drugs and alcohol, and still find something to be grateful for.

Sometimes, you have to lose everything to find gratitude for what you have. If you have a breath, you should be grateful for that. I had to look at my life and realize I wasn't grateful for it, and I was a damn fool for not appreciating what I had.

The Gratitude Game-Changer

Gratitude isn't just some new-age bullshit. It's a powerful tool for transforming your mindset and helping you show up with positivity. But here's the kicker – nobody ever told me I had to practice it. So I didn't know, and that's okay. You know now, and you can start practicing gratefulness to change your mindset.

It's so easy to focus on the negative, to fixate on it until all the good turns to shit in your head. But you can change that. It takes practice, but it's worth it. Start by understanding your negative self-beliefs. Once you understand them, you can reframe them and start practicing changing your language to support a positive mindset.

Life: Punishment or Gift?

For the first portion of my life, I thought life was a punishment. It took me a long time to realize that life is a gift, and you can do with it whatever you want. I didn't know that for the longest time. I thought life was something that was happening to me, not something I could help shape and change.

Here's a truth bomb for you: You don't need permission from anybody to show up with positivity. You should make every effort to do the things you are most passionate about, the things you love to do, to the best of your capability. Take the chances and go after the things you want, regardless of your current conditions. That's what showing up with positivity is all about.

Practical Steps to Mindset Transformation

Alright, enough philosophy. Let's get down to brass tacks. How do we actually transform our mindset to show up with positivity? Here are some practical steps:

1. Identify Your Negative Beliefs: Make a list of the negative beliefs you have about yourself, sobriety, and life in general. Where did these come from? Are they actually true?

2. Challenge and Reframe: For each negative belief, come up with evidence that contradicts it. Then, create a new, more positive belief to replace it.

3. Practice Gratitude: Every day, write down three things you're grateful for. They can be big or small. The point is to train your brain to look for the positive.

4. Embrace Vulnerability: Start small. Share something personal with a trusted friend. Allow yourself to feel your emotions instead of numbing them.

5. Redefine Your Values: What does showing up with positivity mean to you? Write out your new definition and live by it.

6. Mindfulness Practice: Start with just 5 minutes a day. Focus on your breath and observe your thoughts without judgment. This

helps you recognize negative thought patterns so you can shift them.

7. Seek Support: Consider therapy, especially EMDR, if you have trauma. Join support groups where you can be honest about your struggles and learn from others practicing positivity in recovery.

8. Set Meaningful Goals: What do you want to achieve in your sober life? Set specific, achievable goals that align with your new positive outlook.

9. Celebrate Small Wins: Acknowledge every step forward, no matter how small. You're rewriting decades of programming – it takes time.

10. Serve Others: Find ways to help others in recovery. It reinforces your new positive identity and gives you purpose.

The Ongoing Battle

Here's the thing about mindset transformation – it's not a one-and-done deal. It's an ongoing process. You'll have days where negativity creeps back in. That's okay. The key is to recognize it when it happens and redirect yourself back to your new positive mindset.

Remember, you're undoing years, maybe decades, of fucked-up programming. It takes time. Be patient with yourself, but also be persistent. Every time you challenge a negative thought, choose gratitude over self-pity, and face a fear sober, you're rewiring your brain to show up with positivity.

Your Gladiator Homework

1. Read "The Body Keeps the Score" by Bessel van der Kolk. It'll give you a deeper understanding of trauma and how to heal, which is

crucial for maintaining a positive outlook.

2. Start a daily gratitude practice. Write down three things you're grateful for each day.

3. Identify your top three negative self-beliefs. For each one, write out where it came from and evidence that contradicts it. Then, create a positive affirmation to counter each negative belief.

4. Practice vulnerability. Share something personal with someone you trust.

5. Write out your new definition of what it means to show up with positivity.

6. Try a mindfulness app like Headspace or Calm. Start with just 5 minutes a day.

7. Research EMDR therapists in your area. If you have trauma (and let's face it, most of us do), consider giving it a try.

8. Set one meaningful goal for your sober life that aligns with your new positive outlook. Break it down into small, achievable steps.

Conclusion: Your New Positive Warrior Mindset

You've come a long way, Gladiator. From pouring out that last beer to rewiring your brain for positivity, you're not the same person you were when we started this round.

Remember, showing up with positivity is an ongoing process. It's not about perfection. It's about progress. Every day is a chance to strengthen your positive mindset, choose life as a gift rather than a punishment, and be the person you want to be rather than who you thought you had to be.

You've got this, warrior. Your mind is your most powerful weapon in this fight. Use it wisely. Now get out there and show your trauma, your addiction, and anyone who ever doubted you that you can face this world with a positive outlook, even when it's tough as hell.

Round 4 is coming. And trust me, you will want a clear head and a positive warrior's mindset for what's next. Let's fucking do this.

Round 4: Self-Reflection

(OR HOW TO FACE YOUR DEMONS AND MAKE AMENDS)

Alright, Gladiators. You've made it through three rounds. Your mindset's shifting and your resolve is strengthening, but now it's time for the real heavyweight bout: facing yourself and the wreckage of your past.

Welcome to Round 4: Self-Reflection. This is where we dive deep into the cesspool of our past, drag our demons into the light, and learn to face them and make amends for the havoc they've wreaked.

The Core Value: Accepting Responsibility

Let's start with a core value that's going to be your North Star in this shitstorm of self-discovery: Accepting Responsibility.

Now, for some of you (like yours truly, an adopted kid with more baggage than an international airport), this might sound about as appealing as a root canal. But here's the truth: without accepting responsibility, all your self-reflection is just mental masturbation.

Let me tell you a story that'll make this crystal clear.

Picture this: It's a few years back. I'm about two and a half years sober, riding high on my white horse of sobriety. I'm feeling so good I decide to play with fire and try that bullshit called moderation. (Spoiler alert: it doesn't end well.)

So, I'm out with some buddies from my Masonic Lodge. Now, don't get it twisted. Freemasonry and the Shriners are stand-up organizations. But just like any group, you've got your different cliques. And me? I gravitate toward the boys who like to ride motorcycles and close down bars.

We're having a grand old time, drinking, hollering, the whole nine yards. Remember, I'm not supposed to drink much these days. But when I do go out, I go hard. We close down the bar at 2 AM and end up back at my buddy's garage, tinkering with motorcycles and deciding it's a great idea to smoke some pot.

Being the generous guy I am, I offer up some of my medical cannabis. It's totally legal in Missouri, right? No harm, no foul. Or so I thought.

What I didn't know was that when I tossed that bag on the tray, my buddy's wife had decided to spice things up by mixing in some cocaine. Next thing I knew, I was on a roller coaster ride that felt amazing at the moment but was a one-way ticket to Relapseville.

Now, here's where the "accepting responsibility" part comes in. I had zero problems telling my wife what happened. I took full responsibility for my actions. Sounds good, right?

Wrong.

See, I took responsibility, but I didn't have the self-respect or the moral inventory to realize how fucked up the situation really was. I didn't love myself enough to see that I had put myself in serious danger. I had accepted responsibility, but without a moral compass, it was as useless as tits on a bull.

The Ripple Effect of Our Actions

Here's something I didn't understand at the time, but I do now: My wife cared. She cared deeply. But she didn't know how to deal with it. This poor woman lived a life never knowing if her husband was going to live or die if he was going to come home after work or come home at 6 AM. She experienced a tremendous amount of trauma living this life, and it was 100% my fault.

And it wasn't just her. Our kids, our friends, our coworkers - anyone who had to deal with drunk me (which, let's face it, was pretty much everyone) was affected. They all have had negative experiences because of my drinking. Even now that I'm sober, my very existence can trigger their trauma. It doesn't make much sense to us, but we need to be aware of it.

Taking a Fearless Moral Inventory

This is where the rubber meets the road, folks. Taking a fearless moral inventory isn't just about listing all the shit you've done wrong. It's about looking at your actions, motivations, and values (or lack thereof), and being brutally honest about what you see.

Here's how to do it without wanting to crawl into a bottle afterward:

1. Write it all down. The good, the bad, the ugly. Don't sugarcoat it, but don't be a drama queen, either. Just the facts, ma'am.

2. Look for patterns. Are you always the victim in your stories? Do you consistently choose booze over relationships? Do you lie to avoid conflict?

3. Identify your values. What matters to you? What lines won't you

cross? What lines have you already crossed?

4. Face the consequences. For each action, write down how it affected you and others. Be specific.

5. Find the lesson. What can you learn from each situation? How can you use this knowledge to make better choices in the future?

Remember, this isn't about beating yourself up. It's about gaining clarity. You can't change what you don't acknowledge.

The Power of Forgiveness

Now, here's where it gets really tough. Once you've done this inventory, you have to forgive yourself. Really forgive yourself. I don't think you can do that until you know those times are past and you won't fall into the same traps. But once you're there, you have to let go of the guilt and shame.

But it doesn't stop there. You also need to ask for forgiveness from your loved ones. You might get it; you might not. Chances are they will tell you that they forgive you, and they will truly mean it. However, they have trauma that you caused, and if you're really close with this person, you're going to have years, potentially, of flare-ups from these incidents.

Your partner, your children, your coworkers - anyone who has had a negative experience because of your drinking (and trust me, they've had negative experiences) - their trauma can still be triggered by your existence, even though you're not drinking. It doesn't make a whole lot of sense to you, I know. It doesn't need to. But you need to be aware of it.

If you want to maintain the relationships you had during your addiction with the people who were there, who loved you and did their best to support you (even if they didn't have the tools to do it properly), you need to gain their forgiveness. And you need to be patient with the process.

The Ongoing Journey of Healing

Here's the kicker: this isn't a one-and-done deal. You might have to re-apologize. You might have to ask for forgiveness multiple times. You have to not only reshape your perception of yourself and who you are as a human, but you have a lot of work to do to reshape everybody else's perception of who you are.

It's your job now to stand strong. When their trauma gets triggered, when they blame you for things that aren't happening anymore, you need to be there. You need to be understanding. You need to be the rock that you should have been all along.

If you don't want to have relationships with these people, then their opinion of you is their business. Move on, ask forgiveness, hold your head high, and just know that you're living the best life that you can. But if you want these people in your life, you must be prepared for a long journey of rebuilding trust and helping them heal.

Building Self-Love: The Foundation of Change

Here's a trick that might make you cringe at first, but trust me, it works. Every morning, stand in front of the mirror, look yourself in the eye, and say, "I love and respect you."

Yeah, I know. It sounds like some new-age, kumbaya bullshit. But here's the thing: your brain believes what you tell it repeatedly. So, even if you don't believe it at first, even if it feels awkward and uncomfortable, do it anyway.

It might take days, weeks, or even months, but eventually, you'll start to believe it. And when you do, it'll change everything. Because when you truly love and respect yourself, you're less likely to put yourself in situations that compromise your sobriety or integrity.

Putting It All Together: The Power of Self-Reflection and Responsibility

Now, let's bring it all home. Remember those buddies I mentioned earlier? The ones I had that wild night with? Well, something was different the next time they called to go out.

This time, I had done the work. I had taken that fearless moral inventory. I had started to build some self-love and self-respect. So, instead of jumping at the chance to party, I was able to say, "I love you guys, but I just don't think it's healthy for me to hang out with you. I hope you have a great night."

That, my friends, is the power of self-reflection and accepting responsibility. It's not just about admitting when you've fucked up. It's about knowing yourself well enough to make better choices in the first place.

Your Gladiator Homework

So here's your homework, warriors:

1. Start your fearless moral inventory today. Don't hold back. The only person you're cheating if you do is yourself.

2. Write out your core values. Post them somewhere you'll see them every day. Read them every morning.

3. Start the mirror exercise. Yes, it's cheesy. Do it anyway. Your future self will thank you.

4. Make a list of people you need to make amends to. Start with the most important relationships in your life.

5. Begin the process of making amends. Remember, this isn't just about apologizing. It's about acknowledging the hurt you've

caused and asking what you can do to make it right.

6. The next time you're faced with a choice that could compromise your sobriety or your values, pause. Reflect. Ask yourself, "Is this in line with who I want to be?"

7. Find an accountability partner—someone who'll call you on your bullshit and support you in your growth.

Remember, Gladiators, self-reflection without action is just navel-gazing. And accepting responsibility without self-reflection is just empty words. You need both. You deserve both.

You're not just staying sober. You're becoming a person you can be proud to be—a person worthy of love and respect – starting with your own.

So look that demon in the mirror in the eye. Tell it you love it. Mean it. And then go out and live like you mean it.

Round 5 is coming. And trust me, you will want a clear conscience and a heart full of self-love for what's next.

Round 5: Authenticity and Vulnerability

(OR HOW TO STOP WASTING ENERGY ON BULLSHIT AND JUST BE YOU)

ALRIGHT, GLADIATORS. WE'RE FIVE rounds deep into this fight for sobriety, and it's time to get real. Welcome to Round 5: Authenticity and Vulnerability. This is where we strip away the bullshit, drop the masks, and learn to be our genuine selves - warts and all.

The Truth About Authenticity

Let me lay it out for you straight: Being anything other than authentic takes up too much fucking energy. If you're using that much energy to be something you're not, you're more likely to fail on the things you're trying to accomplish in your recovery. You're focusing on the wrong aspects of this journey.

Think about it. How much energy have you wasted trying to be what others expect you to be? How many times have you said "I'm fine" when you're falling apart inside? How often have you gone along with the crowd, even when it felt wrong in your gut? All that pretending, all that hiding - it's exhausting. And in recovery, you need all the energy you can get.

The Early Lessons in Being Different

Let me tell you a personal story about how I first gained the ability to be authentic. It all started in kindergarten. I was a shy kid who couldn't tell my right from my left or read very well. It was obvious I was different. Now, this was 1980, and things were drastically different back then.

I have a high IQ, I'm good at math and science, and I'm good at a lot of things if I have the context. But I'm not good at some very fundamental things. So, right out of the gate, they put me in the Special School District.

I was with the other kids for the first couple of hours each day. But when class started, I had to leave and attend a special needs class. It was a mix of kids - me with dyslexia, some with behavior disorders, Down syndrome, autism. From a very early age, I was used to being pointed at, laughed at, and being different from the norm.

This continued until fourth grade when they allowed me to get out of the Special School District. They held me back a year, thinking I could keep up with the other kids if I repeated the fourth grade on a normal track. But guess what? In fifth and sixth grade, they put me right back into SSD.

The Turning Point

It wasn't until junior high that things started to change. The different structure and extracurricular activities like speech and auto maintenance were game changers for me. But here's the important part: All this allowed me to be myself in that world. People would look at me and laugh anyway, so I learned that what other people thought of me was none of my business.

Remember this, Gladiators: Other people's opinion of you is none of your fucking business.

This lesson was crucial. It taught me that trying to fit in and be "normal" was a waste of time and energy. I was different, and that was okay. In fact, it was more than okay - it was my strength.

The Exhaustion of Pretending in Recovery

Fast forward to early sobriety. The decision to quit drinking for a day or two was easy. Even 30 days wasn't that challenging because I knew I could drink again after. But when I hit the need to go through physical withdrawal, that's when I knew I had a real problem.

Let me tell you, going through withdrawal is no joke. It's like your body is revolting against you, punishing you for daring to quit. The shakes, the sweats, the nausea - it's hell. I had to go through this process a couple of times. Twice for alcohol and once for Xanax. Yeah, that's another whole story.

But here's the thing: As brutal as the physical withdrawal was, it was nothing compared to the mental exhaustion that came after.

Once I was through the physical withdrawal and made the decision to quit drinking, I realized something crucial: The energy I had to spend as a "recovering addict" was exhausting, and it just didn't fucking work.

Acknowledging or having a mindset of "I'm an alcoholic and I'm in recovery" was just something that drained me. It didn't represent who I wanted to be. It didn't represent someone in charge of their own destiny. It's a victim mentality, and it just didn't feel right for me to have this constant state of being "in recovery."

The Problem with the "Recovering Addict" Identity

Let's break this down for a minute. When you constantly identify as a "recovering addict" or an "alcoholic," what are you really saying to yourself? You're saying that you're perpetually broken, perpetually at risk, perpetually one step away from relapse.

Don't get me wrong - acknowledging the problem is important. But there's a big difference between acknowledging your past struggles and defining your entire identity by them.

It's like walking around with a sign that says "I'm damaged goods" plastered to your forehead. How the hell are you supposed to move forward when you're constantly reminding yourself (and everyone around you) of your past?

The Power of Redefining Yourself

So, I had to figure out something else. That's when I figured out how to reclaim sobriety and became a sober man. I redefined who I was as a human, and I could be that authentic self. And let me tell you, it's liberating. It's exciting. It's fun.

This redefinition gives me the power to sit in a bar and not drink. Not because I'm a recovering addict but because I'm a sober person. That's who I am. It's my authentic self.

Think about the difference in mindset. When you're a "recovering addict," every social situation involving alcohol is a test of your willpower. You're constantly on guard, constantly fighting the urge to drink.

But when you're a "sober person," it's just who you are. It's not a daily struggle; it's a choice you've made about who you want to be. It's empowering as hell.

The Journey to Authenticity

Now, I'm not going to bullshit you. Getting to this point isn't easy. It takes work. It takes self-reflection. It takes courage. But it's worth every ounce of effort.

Until you get there and redefine yourself in a way that feels authentic and empowering, you just have to be yourself. Because the energy of being something different than you are will keep you sick; it will keep you in hell. It's not comfortable at all.

You have to be you. If you don't like who you are, learn how to change what you're doing to be a different person. But do it authentically. Do it because it aligns with your values, not because it's what you think others expect of you.

The Power of Language

Here's a simple but powerful change you can make right now: Instead of saying, "Hi, my name is Ken, and I'm an alcoholic," try "Hi, my name is Ken, and I've struggled with alcohol, but today I'm sober."

Feel the difference? One keeps you stuck in an identity centered around alcohol. The other acknowledges your past but focuses on your present choice and strength. It's empowering.

This isn't just semantics. The words we use shape our reality. When you constantly refer to yourself as an alcoholic, you're reinforcing that identity. You're telling your brain, "This is who I am." But when you shift your language to focus on your choices and strength, you create a new narrative for yourself.

The Challenge of Vulnerability

Now, let's talk about the V-word: Vulnerability. For a lot of us, the very idea of being vulnerable makes us want to punch something. And trust me, I get it. I've struggled with aggression for years. It was my go-to move, my shield against the world.

But here's what I learned: That aggression? It was just a mask for my vulnerability. A way to keep people at arm's length so they couldn't see the real me, the scared me, the me that was hurting.

It took a lot of work - self-reflection, learning to love myself, establishing core values - before I could truly be vulnerable. But once I got there? It was like unlocking a superpower.

Here's the thing about vulnerability: It's not weakness. It's the ultimate strength. It takes more courage to open up and be real than it does to hide behind aggression or addiction.

The Risk and Reward of Vulnerability

Being vulnerable means taking a risk. It means opening yourself up to potential hurt, rejection, or judgment. And for those of us who've used alcohol as a shield for so long, that can be terrifying.

But here's the payoff: When you're vulnerable and real with people, they respond. They open up in return. Relationships deepen. Trust grows. You start to build a life that's genuine and fulfilling.

Is it scary? Hell yes. Is it worth it? Abso-fucking-lutely.

Practical Steps to Authenticity

Alright, enough philosophy. Let's get down to brass tacks. How do we actually cultivate authenticity and vulnerability in our lives? Here are some practical steps:

1. Self-Reflection: Take time to really understand who you are, what you value, and what you want from life. This isn't a one-time thing. It's an ongoing process.

2. Honest Communication: Start expressing your true thoughts and feelings, even if it's uncomfortable at first. This doesn't mean being brutally honest all the time. It means being truthful in a respectful way to others and yourself.

3. Set Boundaries: Learn to say no to things that don't align with your authentic self. This is crucial. When you're always saying yes to please others, you're often saying no to yourself.

4. Embrace Your Quirks: Those things that make you different? They're what make you unique. Own them.

5. Practice Self-Compassion: Be kind to yourself. You're on a journey, and it's okay to make mistakes.

6. Reframe Your Identity: Choose language that empowers you rather than defines you by your struggles.

7. Find Your Tribe: Surround yourself with people who accept and encourage your authentic self.

8. Practice Vulnerability: Start small. Share something personal with someone you trust.

9. Mindfulness Practice: Stay present in the moment. Often, we're inauthentic because we're worried about the future or dwelling on the past.

10. Journaling: Keep a journal where you can be completely honest with yourself. No censoring, no judging.

The SMART Approach

Here's something else I've learned: Labels can be limiting. That's why I prefer SMART Recovery over AA. Don't get me wrong, AA has some great tools. But in SMART, instead of saying, "I'm an alcoholic," you say, "I'm Ken, and I struggle with alcohol and aggression."

See the difference? One defines you by your addiction. The other acknowledges your struggles without letting them become your identity. It's a small shift, but it's powerful.

Dealing with Setbacks

There will be times when you slip back into old patterns. Maybe you put on a mask in a social situation. Maybe you avoid being vulnerable when it feels too scary. That's okay. It's part of the process.

The key is recognizing when it happens and gently guiding yourself back to authenticity. Don't beat yourself up. Instead, ask yourself:

- What was I afraid of in that moment?

- What would being authentic have looked like?

- How can I handle a similar situation differently next time?

Each setback is an opportunity to learn and grow. Use them.

Your Homework

Alright, Gladiators, it's time to put this into action. Here's your homework for the next week:

1. Write out your new identity statement. "I am [Your Name], and I am [how you choose to define yourself positively]."

2. Identify one mask you wear - one inauthentic behavior - and commit to dropping it this week.

3. Practice one act of authenticity each day. It can be as simple as honestly expressing how you feel about something.

4. Start a journal where you can be completely honest with yourself.

5. Reframe how you talk about your struggles. Instead of "I am an addict," try "I have struggled with addiction, but I choose sobriety."

6. Have one vulnerable conversation with someone you trust.

7. Identify three of your quirks or unique traits. Write about how these make you who you are.

8. Practice setting one boundary this week.

9. Meditate for 5 minutes each day, focusing on being present with yourself exactly as you are.

10. At the end of the week, write a letter to yourself about what you've learned through these exercises.

Conclusion: Your Authentic Self Awaits

You've come a long way, Gladiator. From pouring out that last drink to peeling off the masks you've worn for so long. It's not an easy journey, but it's one that leads to true freedom.

Remember, authenticity and vulnerability aren't destinations you reach and then you're done. They're ongoing practices. You'll have good days and bad days. The important thing is to keep showing up, being real, and opening up.

You're not just staying sober. You're becoming the realest, rawest, most authentic version of yourself. And let me tell you, that version of you? It's fucking amazing.

Round 6 is coming. And you'll need all the authenticity and vulnerability you can muster for what's next. So drop the bullshit, open your heart, and get ready to get real. You've got this, Gladiator.

Round 6: Discipline and Structure

(OR HOW TO MASTER THE ART OF NOT DOING)

ALRIGHT, GLADIATORS. WE'RE SIX rounds deep into this fight for sobriety, and it's time to talk about something that might make you want to run for the hills: Discipline and Structure. But before you bail, let me tell you this – we're not talking about the kind of discipline you're used to. We're talking about the discipline of not doing. And trust me, for overachievers like us, this might be the hardest thing you've ever done.

The Discipline Dilemma

Let's start with a truth bomb: The discipline to do something isn't the same as the discipline to not do something.

I know many of you are high achievers. You're the type who can pull a 100-hour work week to get a product launched on time. You're a machine when it comes to grinding out tasks and meeting deadlines. And you know what? I believe you. I've been there.

But here's the kicker – that kind of discipline? It's a cakewalk compared to what we're talking about today.

Think about it. Going to lunch with a client and not having a beer? Being really angry and not just going to the bar to blow off some steam? Driving home after a stressful day and not stopping at the gas station for a couple of tall boys? That shit is hard.

See, for high-functioning folks like us, it's easy to understand: "Here's a task; now do it." But when the job is to not do something? That's when it gets tricky.

The Procrastination Paradox

Now, here's where things get interesting. We're about to flip the script on something you've probably been told is a bad habit: procrastination. That's right, in early sobriety, procrastination can be your secret weapon.

Here's how it worked for me. I started by telling myself, "If I want to go to the bar, I have to wait one minute." Just one minute. I'd use that minute to talk myself out of it. Then I bumped it up to 10 minutes. Then 30 minutes. I just kept building it up.

This isn't about never drinking again. It's about not drinking right now. Alcohol will always be there (unfortunately and fortunately). You can tell yourself, "I don't have to drink today. It will be there tomorrow if I relapse tomorrow. But I don't have to relapse right now."

The Dopamine Chair

Let me introduce you to a little trick I call the Dopamine Chair. It's simple, but it's powerful. Here's what you do:

1. Place a chair in your office or living room, somewhere between you and the front door.

2. Any time you have a knee-jerk reaction to do something – like hit the bar – sit in that chair for one minute.

3. Set a timer. One minute. That's all.

4. Have some notes next to the chair reminding you of your goals.

5. As you get stronger, bump that time up to five minutes.

I never had to go past five minutes, but this gave me the skill set of wanting something and not immediately trying to get it. It's like training your impulse control muscle.

The Super Why: Discovering What You're Willing to Sacrifice

Now, Gladiators, it's time to dig deep. We're going to do an exercise called finding your "Super Why." This isn't just about why you want to quit drinking. This is about uncovering your deepest desires and your true passions in life.

Here's how it works:

1. Ask yourself what you truly desire out of life. What are you passionate about?

2. Keep asking "why" to dig deeper. What's driving that desire?

3. Once you've found your core passion or desire, here's where we flip the script.

Most coaches focusing on success in finance or business will ask you what you need to do to accomplish your goal. But we're going to do something different. We're going to ask: What do you have to give up to accomplish this as fast as possible?

Let me share a personal experience. When I did this exercise with my coach, Billy Jean, from Billy Jean's Marketing, I realized that my deepest desire was to ensure my autistic son would be cared for even after my wife and I were gone. I wanted to make sure he wouldn't end up in the same kind of violent lifestyle I started my life in.

And you know what that son of a bitch Billy said to me? With a straight face, he asked, "What do you have to give up to make sure that becomes a reality as quickly as possible?"

It hit me like a ton of bricks. I realized I had to give up drinking entirely. No more moderation games, no more "just one drink." I had to sacrifice that part of my life to achieve what was truly important to me.

Now, I'll be honest – it still took me a couple of years to fully commit to that sacrifice. But that moment of clarity was the beginning of real change for me.

So, Gladiators, I want you to do this exercise. Find your Super Why. Uncover what you're truly passionate about. And then ask yourself – what are you willing to give up to make it happen as quickly as possible?

Embracing Self-Improvement

Now, let's talk about Step 6 of AA: Being entirely ready to have God remove all these defects of character. Whether or not you believe in a higher power, the essence of this step is about being ready for change. It's about acknowledging that there are parts of yourself that need work.

But here's the thing – we're not just passively waiting for these defects to be removed. We're actively working on improving ourselves. This is where that discipline we talked about earlier comes in.

Self-improvement isn't just about adding new skills or habits. It's often about removing the things that no longer serve us. And yeah, that includes alcohol.

Behavioral Activation: Building New Routines

Now, let's borrow a page from Smart Recovery and talk about behavioral activation. This is a fancy term for establishing new routines and habits that support your sobriety.

Here's the deal – when you stop drinking, you're left with a lot of time and energy that you used to spend on alcohol. If you don't fill that time with something positive, you'll likely fall back into old habits.

So, what can you do? Here are some ideas:

1. Exercise: It's good for your body and your mind. Plus, it's a great way to boost those feel-good chemicals in your brain naturally.

2. Meditation or Mindfulness: This can help you deal with cravings and negative emotions.

3. Hobbies: Find something you're passionate about. Maybe it's painting, playing an instrument, or building model airplanes. Whatever it is, dive in.

4. Learning: Take a class, learn a new language, read books. Keep your mind engaged and growing.

5. Volunteering: Helping others can give you a sense of purpose and fulfillment.

The key is to create a routine that supports your sobriety. Wake up at the same time every day. Plan your meals. Schedule time for self-care and recovery activities.

Being Organized and Disciplined

Now, let's connect all this to our core value of being organized and disciplined. This isn't about turning you into a robot or sucking all the spontaneity out of your life. It's about creating a framework that supports your goals and your sobriety.

Here's how to put this into practice:

1. Set Clear Goals: Use the insights from your Super Why exercise to set meaningful goals. What do you want to achieve in your sobriety? In your life?

2. Break It Down: Take those big goals and break them down into smaller, actionable steps.

3. Create a Schedule: Plan out your days and weeks. Include time for work, recovery activities, self-care, and fun.

4. Use Tools: Find tools that work for you. Maybe it's a planner, a to-do list app, or a wall calendar. Use whatever helps you stay organized.

5. Review and Adjust: Regularly review your progress. What's working? What isn't? Be willing to adjust your approach as needed.

6. Follow Through: This is where the rubber meets the road. When you commit to something, do it. Build that trust with yourself.

Remember, Gladiators, discipline isn't about punishment. It's about freedom—the freedom to choose your actions rather than being a slave to your impulses.

Your Gladiator Homework

Alright, warriors, it's time to put this into action. Here's your homework for the next week:

1. Do the Super Why Exercise: Dig deep. Find your core passion. Then, ask yourself what you need to give up to achieve it as quickly as possible.

2. Set Up Your Dopamine Chair: Designate a spot for your one-minute (or five-minute) cool-down sessions.

3. Create a Daily Routine: Design a routine that supports your sobriety. Include time for self-care, recovery activities, and pursuing your passions.

4. Practice the Discipline of Not Doing: Next time you feel an urge to drink or act out, use your Dopamine Chair. Start with one minute and work your way up.

5. Set One Meaningful Goal: Based on your Super Why, set one significant goal for your recovery or your life. Break it down into actionable steps.

6. Start a New Positive Habit: Choose one small habit to incorporate into your daily routine that supports your sobriety.

7. Identify One Thing to Give Up: Based on your Super Why, what's one thing you can give up this week that's holding you back from your goals?

Conclusion: The Disciplined Gladiator

Remember, Gladiators, discipline and structure aren't about restricting your freedom. They're about creating the freedom to live the life you truly want.

You're not just staying sober. You're building a life of purpose, a life of achievement, a life you can be proud of. And sometimes, that means having the discipline not to do something, even when every fiber of your being is screaming to do it.

But you know what? You've got this. You're a fucking Gladiator. You're stronger than you know, more resilient than you believe, and more badass than you can imagine.

So get out there and show the world what a disciplined, structured, sober warrior looks like. Because Round 7 is coming, and you'll need all the discipline you can muster for what's next.

Stay strong, stay structured, and keep fighting the good fight, Gladiators. I'll see you in the next round.

Round 7: Cultivating Calmness

(OR HOW TO STOP BEING A TICKING TIME BOMB AND FIND YOUR ZEN)

ALRIGHT, GLADIATORS. WE'RE SEVEN rounds deep into this fight for sobriety, and it's time to talk about something that might seem counterintuitive to your warrior spirit: calmness. That's right, we're going to learn how to cultivate inner peace in a world that seems hellbent on pissing you off. Welcome to Round 7: Cultivating Calmness.

The Buddha's Truth Bomb

Before we dive in, let me drop some ancient wisdom on you. The Buddha, that OG of inner peace, laid out four noble truths that are as relevant to your recovery as they are to life in general:

1. There is suffering.

2. There is a cause of suffering.

3. There is an end to suffering.

4. There is a path that leads to the end of suffering.

Now, I know what you're thinking. "No shit, Sherlock. I'm in recovery. I know all about suffering." But hang with me here because understanding these truths is key to cultivating the calmness we're after.

The Aggression Trap

Let me tell you, staying calm and building positive relationships was so fucking hard for me. It's still where I fail most frequently. I'm a passionate man, and over my life, I've been rewarded for my aggressions more than I've been punished for them.

Face it: in our world, being aggressive pays. The most violent country wins. The person who can take and hold the land is the conqueror. The winner writes the story. Everything around us rewards aggressive behavior.

But here's the kicker: that aggression doesn't do you any good in the sobriety game. It's not going to help you stay calm or build positive relationships. And those two things? They're fucking crucial to your recovery.

The Calm Before the Storm (of Sobriety)

I'm not saying you need to become some zen master overnight. But learning to cultivate calmness is like learning to breathe underwater. It might feel unnatural at first, but it's a skill that can save your life.

When I found out I had liver disease and had to quit drinking, I needed something to keep me distracted. That's when I turned to boxing. Yeah, you heard me right. I turned to a combat sport to find peace. Life's funny that way.

I started with heavy bag boxing, which led me to compete at the amateur level in the Golden Gloves. And let me tell you, those first few sparring sessions were a wake-up call. I'd get hit, get frustrated, start moving forward recklessly, and make mistakes. And in boxing, every mistake comes with an instant reminder - a punch to the face.

It was my first real experience trying to stay calm and build positive relationships in high-stress situations. I realized that if I wanted to learn and improve, I needed to stay calm even when someone was trying to knock my block off.

The Breath of Life (and Sobriety)

That's when I started exploring breathing techniques and going to yoga classes. I needed to figure out how to compete at a high level while staying calm. It was the only way I could learn the skills and techniques to move forward in boxing.

But here's the beautiful thing: those same breathing techniques that helped me in the ring? They started helping me in every area of my life. I use them at work with my team when I get frustrated and need to explain something for the twentieth time. I use them when my wife and I are arguing. I use them when I'm faced with a challenging situation that in the past would have sent me reaching for a bottle.

Two techniques, in particular, have been game-changers for me:

1. Box Breathing: Inhale for a count of 5, hold for 5, exhale for 5, and hold for 5. Repeat. Ten rounds

2. The 4-8 Method: Inhale through your nose on a 4 count and Exhale slowly through your month for an 8 count. Ten rounds.

There are links to VIdes in the Resources section of this book, but for now, just know that your breath is a powerful tool in your calmness arsenal.

The Trigger Warning (That Actually Helps)

Here's something I realized along the way: one of my biggest triggers for drinking was anger. When I'd get mad, I'd want to drink because that seemed like the quickest way to feel good again and move on.

So, I had to learn not to let myself get all worked up in the first place. It was about catching the spark before it turned into a wildfire. And that's where the breathing exercises came in clutch.

By practicing these techniques regularly, I started to catch myself earlier in the anger cycle. Instead of going from zero to rage in 2.5 seconds, I could feel the anger building and use my breath to defuse it.

The Relationship Renovation

Now, let's talk about relationships. When you're in active addiction, your relationships are about as healthy as a Big Mac diet. But here's the thing: You need those key players in your life to help you recover.

The problem is, we've been drinking for a long time. The people who've stuck around? They love us, but the relationship is challenging, to say the least. And that's where staying calm comes in handy again.

Using the breathing techniques I learned through yoga and boxing, I started applying them to my relationships. When arguing with my wife or dealing with a challenging coworker, I'd use these techniques to stay calm and communicate more effectively.

The Energy Equation

Here's a hard truth: maintaining negative relationships will cost you. For some reason, we want to make it work. We think that showing we can turn a relationship around is empowering. But at the end of the day, if you can't build a positive relationship with the people around you, the stress and energy it takes to be around that person is going to be too much. And that increases your chances of relapsing.

It's like trying to run a marathon while carrying a backpack full of rocks. You might make it, but why make it harder on yourself?

The Spiritual Side of Calmness

Now, you may not see it from the outside, but I'm a fairly spiritual person. I always have been. I practice something called pantheism. I don't believe in a single religion, but I believe that whatever you believe in, whatever religion you practice, the phrase "what is held true above will be held true below" will always be the case.

So if you believe Jesus is your savior, that is absolutely true for you, and that belief will help you through. If you believe in the power of the universe, Allah, or the Flying Spaghetti Monster, that's cool, too. The point is that spiritual practice can be a powerful tool in cultivating calmness.

The Magic Rock (No, Really)

Here's where things might get a little "hippy-dippy" for some of you, but stick with me. A good friend of mine, Tracy, once gave me a black tourmaline stone. She told me that if I meditated with it and rubbed it, it would remove negative people from my life - the people who were blocking me.

Now, I was skeptical. But I figured, what the hell, I'll give it a shot. And you know what? After a couple of months of this practice, I noticed changes. People who I thought were important to me but who were actually creating harm in my life started to drift away.

At first, I thought, "Damn, that rock works too well!" But over time, I realized that these relationships had been draining me, keeping me in a negative mindset that made me want to drink.

The Relationship Detox

Here's the thing about cultivating calmness and building positive relationships: sometimes, it means letting go of the negative ones. And I'm not going to sugarcoat it - this can be fucking hard.

These might be people you love - ex-coworkers, partners, family members, fraternity brothers. And you might still love them. But if they can't be part of your regular life in a positive way, if being around them threatens your calmness and your sobriety, you need to create some distance.

It doesn't have to be forever. You can try to bring them back into your life when you're healthier and stronger in your recovery. But for now, you need to prioritize your calmness and your sobriety.

The Calmness Toolkit

Alright, Gladiators, now that we've laid the groundwork, let's talk about some practical tools you can use to cultivate calmness in your life:

1. Meditation: I know, I know. You're thinking, "I'm not some monk sitting on a mountain." But trust me, meditation is a game-changer. Start small - even 5 minutes a day can make a difference. And if you can swing it, I highly recommend the Muse headset. It's like a personal trainer for your brain.

2. Breathing Exercises: We touched on these earlier, but they're worth repeating. Box breathing and the 4-8 method are my go-to techniques. Practice them daily, and they'll be there for you when you need them most.

3. Mindfulness: This is about being present in the moment. When you're washing dishes, wash dishes. When you're walking, walk. It's about getting out of your head and into your life.

4. Physical Exercise: Boxing worked for me, but find what works for you. Running, weightlifting, yoga - whatever gets you moving and

helps you release that pent-up energy.

5. Journaling: Writing down your thoughts and feelings can be a powerful way to process them and find calm.

6. Nature Time: Spend time outdoors. There's something inherently calming about being in nature.

7. Gratitude Practice: Write down three things you're grateful for each day. It's hard to be stressed when you're feeling thankful.

8. Healthy Sleep Habits: Never underestimate the power of a good night's sleep for maintaining calmness.

9. Healthy Eating: What you put in your body affects your mind. Eat well to feel well.

10. Spiritual Practice: Whatever this means for you - prayer, meditation, reading spiritual texts. Connecting to something bigger than yourself can bring a sense of peace.

The Gladiator's Guide to Calmness

Now, I know what you're thinking. "Ken, this all sounds great, but how does being calm fit with being a Sobriety Gladiator? Aren't gladiators supposed to be fierce warriors?"

Here's the thing: the fiercest warriors aren't the ones who are always raging. They're the ones who can stay calm in the heat of battle. They're the ones who can think clearly when everything's going to shit around them.

Being a Sobriety Gladiator isn't about being aggressive or always on the attack. It's about being strong, resilient, and in control. And you know what? It takes much more strength to stay calm in the face of adversity than it does to fly off the handle.

Think about it this way: In the arena of life, you will face many opponents. Cravings, triggers, negative people, stressful situations - they're all coming for you. But if you can stay calm and keep your cool when everything around you is in chaos, that's when you're truly unbeatable.

The Calmness Challenge

Alright, Gladiators, it's time to put this into practice. Here's your homework for the next week:

1. Start daily meditation practice. Start with just 5 minutes a day and work your way up.

2. Practice box breathing or the 4-8 method at least thrice daily.

3. Identify one negative relationship in your life. Reflect on how it affects your calmness and your sobriety. What steps can you take to improve this relationship or create some healthy distance?

4. Start a gratitude journal. Each night before bed, write down three things you're grateful for.

5. The next time you feel angry or stressed, pause and take three deep breaths before responding.

6. Spend at least 30 minutes in nature this week. Pay attention to how it affects your mood.

7. Identify your top three stress triggers. For each one, come up with a calmness strategy.

8. Practice mindfulness during one routine activity each day (like brushing your teeth or washing dishes).

9. Have a calm, honest conversation with someone you trust about your recovery journey.

10. At the end of the week, reflect on how these practices have affected your overall sense of calmness and wellbeing.

The Calm Warrior

Remember, Gladiators, cultivating calmness doesn't mean becoming passive or weak. It means becoming stronger, more resilient, more in control. It means being able to face life's challenges with a clear head and a steady heart.

You're not just staying sober. You're becoming a calm warrior, a person who can weather any storm without losing their shit. And let me tell you, that kind of strength? It's fucking unbeatable.

As you progress in your recovery, keep this in mind: Your calmness is your superpower. It's what will keep you sober when life tries to knock you off course. It's what's going to help you build the positive relationships that will support your new life.

So take a deep breath, Gladiator. Center yourself. Find your calm. Because Round 8 is coming, and you're going to need all the inner peace you can muster for what's next.

You've got this, warrior. Now, go out there and show the world what true strength looks like.

Round 8: Taking Action

(OR HOW TO STOP TALKING AND START DOING)

ALRIGHT, GLADIATORS. WE'RE EIGHT rounds deep into this fight for sobriety, and it's time to put up or shut up. Welcome to Round 8: Taking Action. This is where we stop talking about what we're going to do and start doing it. Our core value for this round? Don't talk about it, be about it.

Now, I know some of you might be expecting me to dive into Step 8 of AA, making a list of all the people we've harmed and becoming willing to make amends. But here's the thing – I don't see the benefit in digging up old bones and reopening old wounds. If that works for you, fantastic. Go for it. But it's not part of my program and doesn't have to be part of yours, either.

Here's why: I've been harming people my entire life. I don't even know where I'd start making that list. And more importantly, I don't see how rehashing all that old pain helps me or anyone else move forward. In my book, it's all about moving forward, not getting stuck in the past.

The Forward-Focused Fighter

Think about it this way: In boxing, when you're in the ring, you don't have time to dwell on the punch you just missed or the hit you just took. You're focused on the next move, the next punch, the next round. That's how we need to approach our sobriety.

So, instead of making lists of past wrongs, we will focus on taking action now. We're going to build the skill of following through on what we say we will do. Because in this ring, your word is your bond – especially to yourself.

The Power of Conviction

In boxing, when you say you will take a fight, you take the fight. Period. There's no hemming and hawing, no "well, maybe I will, maybe I won't." You commit, and you follow through.

We need to bring that same level of conviction to our sobriety. When you say, "I'm going to quit drinking," then by God, you quit drinking. It's about building that unshakeable resolve, that unwavering commitment to your word.

Now, I know what you're thinking. "But Ken, I've tried to quit before and failed. How is this time any different?" And that's a fair question. But here's the thing – those past attempts? They were practice rounds. Now, we're in the main event, and it's time to fight like your life depends on it. Because, guess what? It does.

Building the Action Muscle

The trick I tell my boxing students – and the same applies to you, Sobriety Gladiators – is to build resilience by creating a direct pathway in your brain between saying you'll do something and immediately doing it.

In the last round, we talked about procrastination as a tool, which still applies when dealing with cravings. But this is about building the habit of following through on your commitments, no matter how small.

Start simple. Every morning, before you go into the bathroom, say out loud to yourself, "I'm going to go brush my teeth." Then, immediately walk in and brush your teeth. It sounds trivial, I know. But you're building a crucial neural pathway. You're teaching your brain that when you say you'll do something, you do it. No hesitation, no excuses.

The Trust Fall

Let's talk about trust for a minute. We all have that one friend or family member who's always making promises they don't keep, right? Over time, your trust in that person erodes. You stop believing them when they say they'll do something.

Well, guess what? The same thing happens in your relationship with yourself. Every time you say you're going to do something and don't follow through, you're chipping away at your self-trust. And in recovery, self-trust is everything.

This isn't about never failing. It's not about saying you'll build a house and then beating yourself up when you run out of money halfway through. It's about taking the action you said you would take, giving it your best effort, no matter what.

Breaking It Down

Now, let's say you've got a big goal. Maybe you want to make a million dollars. That's great, but it's not actionable on its own. You need to break it down into smaller, concrete steps.

So instead of just saying, "I'm going to make a million dollars," you might say, "I'm going to start a business that sells widgets." Then you break that down further: "Today, I'm going to research widget manufacturers." Or "This week, I'm going to write a business plan."

The same goes for your sobriety. Don't just say, "I'm never going to drink again." That's too big, too abstract. Instead, say, "I'm not going to drink today." Or even, "If I want to take a drink, I'm going to wait 15 minutes and think it through first."

The Mindset Shift

Here's a truth bomb for you: The day you change your mindset from being an addict to being a sober person, your life starts to get better. I promise you, after the first year and a half to two years of being sober, things get a lot better. But that mindset shift? That can happen right now.

It's a hard change; I'm not going to lie. When you first start telling yourself, "I'm a sober person," you might not believe it. That's okay. Remember, we're building a muscle here. You're training yourself to do what you say you will do, no matter what.

The Small Wins

So, how do we build this muscle? We start small. We've talked about the toothbrush trick. Here's another one: the bedtime commitment. When it's time for bed, say out loud, "I'm going to go to bed now." Then do it. Don't play another round of Candy Crush. Don't watch another episode of your favorite show. Turn off the TV, put down the phone, and go to bed.

These might seem like insignificant actions, but they're not. Each time you follow through on what you say you'll do, you're building trust in yourself. You're proving to yourself that you're a person of your word.

The Mental Workout

We don't often think about exercising our minds and habits, but that's exactly what we're doing here. And let me tell you, it's a beautiful thing when you start to see results.

This is all about learning to trust yourself. But here's the catch – before you can trust yourself, you have to be a trustworthy person to yourself. And that means building up a track record of wins.

The good news? You've got plenty of opportunities for small wins every single day. Every time you say you'll do something and then do it – whether it's brushing your teeth, going to bed on time, or not taking that drink – you're logging another win.

The Gladiator's Guide to Taking Action

Alright, warriors, it's time to put this into practice. Here's your action plan for becoming a person who doesn't just talk but does:

1. The Morning Declaration: Every morning, as soon as you wake up, say out loud, "I am a sober person, and I will not drink today." Then follow through.

2. The Toothbrush Challenge: For the next week, practice the toothbrush trick every single day. Say you'll brush your teeth, then immediately do it.

3. The Bedtime Commitment: Each night, declare your intention to go to bed, then do it immediately.

4. The 15-Minute Rule: If you feel the urge to drink, tell yourself, "I will wait 15 minutes before making a decision." Then do it. Use that time to think it through, call a support person, or distract yourself.

5. The Daily Goal: Each morning, set one small, achievable goal for the day. Say it out loud, write it down, and then make sure you do it.

6. The Weekly Challenge: At the start of each week, choose one slightly bigger goal. Break it down into daily actions, commit to

them out loud, and follow through.

7. The Accountability Report: Review your commitments and actions at the end of each day. Be honest with yourself. Celebrate your wins and learn from any misses.

8. The Habit Tracker: Start a simple habit tracker. List the habits you want to build (including sobriety) and check them off each day you follow through.

9. The Power Hour: Dedicate one hour daily to working toward a bigger goal. Declare what you'll work on at the start of the hour, then do it.

10. The Sobriety Log: Keep a daily log of your sobriety. Each day, write down one thing you did to support your sobriety, no matter how small.

The Action-Oriented Mindset

Remember, Gladiators, this isn't just about sobriety. This is about becoming a person of action in every area of your life. It's about closing the gap between what you say and what you do.

When you become known as someone who follows through – to yourself and others – your whole life changes: opportunities open up, relationships improve, and self-respect skyrockets.

But it all starts with those small, daily actions. It starts with being a person who doesn't just talk about brushing their teeth or going to bed on time but actually does it. Because if you can master those small commitments, the big ones become much less daunting.

The Pitfalls to Watch For

Now, I'm not going to sugarcoat it. This path isn't always easy. There are pitfalls you need to watch out for:

1. The Overpromise Trap: Don't fall into the trap of making grand declarations you can't follow through on. Start small. Build up.

2. The All-or-Nothing Mentality: Remember, this isn't about perfection. If you miss a commitment, don't throw in the towel. Recommit and keep going.

3. The Excuse Factory: Your mind will try to come up with all sorts of reasons why you can't follow through. Recognize these for what they are – excuses – and push past them.

4. The Comfort Zone Clutch: Taking action often means stepping out of your comfort zone. Don't let the fear of discomfort hold you back.

5. The Overwhelm Overload: If you find yourself freezing up because a task seems too big, break it down into smaller, manageable steps.

6. The Validation Void: Don't wait for others to validate your actions. Do it for yourself.

7. The Procrastination Pretense: While strategic procrastination can be useful, be honest with yourself about when you're just putting something off unnecessarily.

The Gladiator's Creed

As we wrap up this round, I want you to internalize this creed:

"I am a Sobriety Gladiator. My words and my actions are one. What I say, I do. What I commit to, I follow through on. I don't just talk about sobriety

– I live it, one action at a time. I am becoming the person I want to be, one promise kept at a time. I don't just fight – I win by doing what needs to be done when it needs to be done."

Repeat this to yourself daily. Let it sink into your bones. Let it become who you are.

The Action Homework

Alright, Gladiators, it's time to put all this into practice. Here's your homework for the next week:

1. Morning Mantra: Start each day by saying aloud, "I am a sober person, and I will not drink today." Then follow through.

2. Action Audit: At the end of each day, write down three things you said you would do and did. If you can't think of three, you know what you need to work on tomorrow.

3. Commitment Calendar: Get a calendar, and each day, write down one small commitment for the next day. Make sure you do it.

4. Victory Log: Start a "victory log" where you write down each commitment you keep, no matter how small.

5. Challenge Chase: Set one slightly challenging goal for the week. Break it down into daily actions. Commit to each action out loud, then do it.

6. Trigger Plan: Identify your top three drinking triggers. For each one, create and write down a specific action plan. When the trigger hits, immediately take the planned action.

7. Accountability Ally: Find an accountability partner. Share your daily commitments with them and report back on your

follow-through.

8. Habit Stack: Choose one existing habit (like brushing your teeth) and stack a new, sobriety-supporting habit on top of it. Commit to it out loud each time.

9. Do-Not-Do List: Write a list of actions that don't support your sobriety. Commit to not doing these things, one day at a time.

10. Action Affirmations: Write down three affirmations that reinforce your identity as a person of action. Repeat these out loud each morning and evening.

Conclusion: The Action-Oriented Gladiator

Remember, Gladiators, in this arena of life, it's not enough to say you'll fight. You have to actually step into the ring. It's not enough to talk about sobriety. You have to live it, one action at a time.

You're not just trying to stay sober. You're becoming a person of your word, a person of action, a person who follows through. You're becoming someone you can trust and, in turn, someone others can trust.

This journey isn't always going to be easy. There will be days when following through feels impossible. But remember – you're a fucking Gladiator. You're stronger than you know, more capable than you believe, and more badass than you can imagine.

So get out there and show the world what a sober, action-oriented warrior looks like. Because Round 9 is coming, and you'll need all the follow-through you can muster for what's next.

Don't just talk about it, be about it, Gladiators. I'll see you in the next round.

Round 9: Making Amends

(OR HOW TO BECOME A WORLD-CLASS HUMAN)

ALRIGHT, GLADIATORS. WE'RE IN the ninth round of this fight for sobriety, and it's time to talk about making amends. But hold on to your hats because we will approach this a little differently than you might expect.

In AA, Step 9 is all about making direct amends wherever possible. In Recovery Dharma, they talk about there being an end to struggle and suffering, cultivating empathy. But here's the thing - we're not just going to focus on the past. We're going to talk about how to make amends by becoming the best damn version of yourself possible.

The World-Class Mindset

Let me introduce you to a core value that I straight-up stole (with permission) from my friend Billy Jean. It's simple but powerful: Genius is a synonym for world-class. At my boxing school, BoxSTL, we say we're a synonym for world-class. We operate like it in everything we do.

Now, I want you to think about what being world-class means to you. What area of your life do you want to excel in? What would it mean to be world-class in your recovery, relationships, and career?

Here's the kicker - once you decide what world-class means to you, you need to tell yourself every single day that you are that thing. It's not about faking it till you make it. It's about setting a standard for yourself and living up to it every damn day.

The Power of Personal Mantras

Now, let's talk about personal mantras. These aren't just feel-good phrases you repeat mindlessly. These powerful statements define who you are and who you're becoming.

My personal mantra has evolved over time. Currently, it's this:

"I am an understanding husband, emotionally available to my children, and grateful for all that fills my life. I deserve great things."

Notice something? There's no mention of being strong, or tough, or any of that macho bullshit. Why? Because I realized that wasn't serving me. In my drinking days, I was using alcohol to protect my emotions, to put up a barrier between me and the world. But that left me unable to truly connect with the people I love.

Your mantra needs to be powerful. No wishy-washy words like "want" or "try." This is about who you are and who you're committed to being. It needs to reflect what you really want in life.

The Evolution of Self

Let me tell you, this shit isn't easy. It takes time, and it takes honesty. My mantra has changed recently, in early 2024. Life threw some serious curveballs my way, things I wasn't prepared for. I won't get into the details here, but it was another turning point.

I realized I was still focusing on the wrong things. I didn't drink through this challenging moment, but fuck, did I want to. I didn't because of the tools I'd built up to that point - tools we've talked about in this book.

Here's a truth bomb for you: There will be a moment in your life that challenges you to your core. You might lose a child, a parent, or a partner. You might face a health crisis or a financial disaster. And when that moment comes, you need to be ready.

The Armor of Self-Love

This is why self-love is so crucial. It's your first line of defense against the shit life throws at you. But here's something I've learned: self-love alone isn't always enough.

In my opinion, if you're not working for some external force or some higher purpose, you're going to have a really hard time recovering. I'm not talking about religion here. I'm not saying you need to believe in Jesus, Buddha, or anyone else. And I'm definitely not saying you should quit drinking for your spouse or your kids - that shit never works.

What I'm talking about is finding a cause, a purpose that's bigger than yourself. Something that will keep you going even in your darkest moments.

The Dark Night of the Soul

See, we alcoholics, we're pretty good at telling ourselves to fuck off. We've spent so long hollowing ourselves out that it's easy to fall back into self-destructive patterns. Even when we're sober, that voice is still there, whispering that we don't need anything or anyone.

And let's be real - being an alcoholic doesn't necessarily mean you hate yourself. But it sure as hell isn't an act of self-love. Any self-injury, whether it's drinking or something else, is not done out of love.

So when you're in those dark moods, those moments when everything feels hopeless, you need to know what you're living for. This is where your personal mantra comes in.

The Logic of World-Class

The phrase "world-class" works because if you identify as a world-class human, you won't engage in self-destructive behavior. Logically, someone who's world-class wouldn't do that shit.

But here's the rub - logic isn't always our best friend when we're in an emotionally distressed place. That's why I don't recommend using "world-class" as your personal mantra. You need something more immediate, more emotional, something that bypasses your logical brain and speaks directly to your heart.

The External Force

We're trying to create an external force that helps you in your darkest days. Something that you instantly know you need to live for. That's why we say these mantras daily or as often as possible.

Now, I'm not saying you need to get up and read a book every day. Start small. For the first couple of days, just look in the mirror and say, "I love and respect you." Then, whenever you see yourself in the mirror, give yourself a quick "I love you, buddy."

As you get comfortable with that, start working on your daily mantra. Maybe do both for a while. Eventually, the "I love and respect you" can become less frequent, and you can focus on your personal mantra.

The Power of Practice

Here's the thing - you don't have to do this every single day of your life. When things are going well, you might not feel the need. But the more you practice, the more ingrained it becomes.

And that's the whole point. We practice these mantras so that in our darkest moments when everything else has gone to shit, these words come to mind first. They become our lifeline.

If you can do these things during meditation and embed them in your subconscious, even better. Not everyone's there yet, and that's okay. Looking yourself in the eyes and saying these affirmations out loud is powerful.

You can do them in the moments before you fall asleep or right when you wake up. The goal is to sink them into your subconscious so that when all logic is gone and you're at your absolute worst, these words catch you.

The Power of External Forces

Trust me, I've been there. From jail cells to being bloodied and battered to sleeping in storm drains - I've seen some dark fucking places. And in those moments, having those external forces, those things you're living for can be the difference between giving up and keeping on.

So, Gladiators, it's time to get to work. It's time to define what world-class means to you. It's time to craft your personal mantra. It's time to find your higher purpose.

Making Amends Through Excellence

Now, you might be wondering how all this ties into making amends. Here's how: The best way to make amends for your past is to live a life of excellence and integrity from now on.

Sure, if there are specific people you've hurt and you can make it right, do it. But don't get stuck in the past. Don't wallow in guilt and shame. Instead, focus on becoming the kind of person who doesn't need to make amends because you're living right every damn day.

This is what I call "living amends." It's about showing up every day as the best version of yourself. It's about being that understanding husband, that emotionally available parent, that grateful human being. It's about being world-class in everything you do.

The Path to World-Class Recovery

So, how do we put all this into practice? How do we become world-class in our recovery? Here's your action plan, Gladiators:

1. Define Your World-Class: What does being world-class mean to you in the context of recovery? Write it down. Be specific.

2. Craft Your Mantra: Create a personal mantra that reflects who you want to be. Remember, no weak words. Make it powerful.

3. Mirror Work: Look yourself in the eye every morning and say your mantra out loud. Mean it.

4. Find Your Purpose: What cause or purpose is bigger than yourself? What would you be willing to stay sober for, no matter what?

5. Daily Reflection: At the end of each day, ask yourself: "Did I show up as a world-class person today?" If not, how can you do better tomorrow?

6. Continuous Learning: Commit to learning something new about recovery every week. Read books, attend meetings, and listen to podcasts. World-class people never stop learning.

7. Help Others: Find ways to help others in their recovery journey. Teaching others reinforces your own learning and gives you a sense of purpose.

8. Physical Excellence: Treat your body like it belongs to a world-class athlete. Eat well, exercise, and get enough sleep.

9. Emotional Intelligence: Work on understanding and managing your emotions. A world-class recovery involves emotional sobriety, too.

10. Gratitude Practice: Every day, write down three things you're grateful for. Gratitude is a hallmark of world-class humans.

The World-Class Mindset in Action

Let me break this down for you with some real-life scenarios:

Scenario 1: The Trigger Situation: You're at a work event, and everyone's drinking. In the past, you would have been first at the bar. But you're world-class now. So, instead of focusing on what you're missing out on, you focus on making meaningful connections. You leave the event having had great conversations and maybe even some new business opportunities.

Scenario 2: The Emotional Crisis: You've just had a massive fight with your partner. In the past, this would have been a perfect excuse to drink. But you're world-class now. Instead, you take a moment to breathe, to center yourself. You remind yourself of your mantra. Then, you approach your partner with empathy and a willingness to understand their perspective. You work through the issue together, strengthening your relationship in the process.

Scenario 3: The Professional Setback: You've just lost a big client or missed a promotion. Old you would have drowned your sorrows.

World-class you? You see this as an opportunity for growth. You analyze what went wrong, make a plan to improve, and come back stronger. You use this setback as fuel for your next success.

Scenario 4: The Social Pressure: You're at a friend's wedding, and everyone's pushing you to have "just one drink" to toast the couple. World-class you will stand firm in your conviction. You toast with your sparkling water, proud of your choice and strength. You enjoy the wedding fully present, creating memories you'll actually remember the next day.

The Challenges of World-Class Recovery

Now, I'm not going to bullshit you. This world-class journey isn't always going to be smooth sailing. You're going to face challenges. You're going to have days where you feel anything but world-class. That's okay. That's normal. What matters is how you handle those moments.

Challenge 1: The Voice of Doubt: There will be times when that little voice in your head tells you you're not world-class and that you're just faking it. When that happens, remind yourself of how far you've come. Look at your gratitude journal. Repeat your mantra. Remember, being world-class isn't about being perfect. It's about constantly striving to be better.

Challenge 2: The Complacency Trap: As you start to succeed in your recovery, it's easy to get complacent. To think you've got this all figured out. That's when you're most vulnerable. World-class recovery means staying vigilant, always working on yourself and striving to improve.

Challenge 3: The Comparison Game: In this age of social media, it's easy to fall into the trap of comparing yourself to others. Remember, your only competition is the person you were yesterday. Focus on your progress, your journey.

Challenge 4: The Overwhelm Overload: Sometimes, the idea of being "world-class" in everything can feel overwhelming. When that happens, break it down. Focus on being world-class in this moment, this decision, this action—one step at a time.

The Ripple Effect of World-Class Recovery

Here's something beautiful about this world-class approach to recovery: it doesn't just change you. It changes everything and everyone around you.

When you show up as your best self every day and live with integrity and excellence, you inspire others. Your kids see what real strength looks like. Your partner experiences what true emotional availability feels like. Your colleagues witness what genuine professionalism is.

This is how you make amends. Not by dwelling on the past but by creating a better future. Be the kind of person who uplifts others just by being in their presence.

The World-Class Recovery Toolkit

Alright, Gladiators, it's time to equip you with some specific tools for your world-class recovery journey:

1. The Morning Power Hour: Start your day with purpose. Spend 20 minutes on physical exercise, 20 minutes on reading or learning, and 20 minutes on meditation or reflection. This sets the tone for a world-class day.

2. The Emotion Wheel: Get yourself an emotion wheel (you can find these online). Whenever you're feeling off, use this to identify exactly what you're feeling. World-class emotional intelligence starts with accurate identification.

3. The Victory Log: Keep a daily log of your victories, no matter how small. Did you resist a craving? Log it. Did you have a meaningful conversation? Log it. This builds your confidence and reinforces your world-class identity.

4. The Stress Resilience Routine: Develop a go-to routine for when stress hits. This might include deep breathing, a quick walk, or listening to a specific song. Having this routine ready makes you resilient in the face of stress.

5. The Growth Mindset Mantra: When faced with a challenge, repeat to yourself: "This is an opportunity for growth." This transforms obstacles into opportunities.

6. The Accountability Partner: Find someone who's also committed to world-class living. Check in with each other regularly. Support each other. Challenge each other.

7. The Integrity Check: At the end of each day, ask yourself: "Did my actions align with my values today?" If not, plan how to do better tomorrow.

8. The Forgiveness Practice: Regularly practice forgiveness for others and yourself. This keeps you from getting stuck in resentment or shame.

9. The Skill Stack: Continuously work on building new skills that support your recovery. This might be stress management techniques, communication skills, or hobby-related skills that bring you joy.

10. The Inspiration Bank: Keep a collection of quotes, stories, or images that inspire you to be your best self. Turn to these when you need a motivational boost.

The World-Class Recovery Pledge

As we wrap up this round, I want you to make a pledge to yourself. Repeat after me:

"I, [Your Name], commit to world-class recovery. I promise to show up every day as the best version of myself. I will face my challenges with courage and grace. I will treat myself and others with respect and compassion. I will continuously learn and grow. I will use my recovery to inspire and uplift others. I am world-class, and I live up to that standard every day."

Your World-Class Homework

1. Craft Your World-Class Definition: Write out what being world-class in recovery means to you. Be specific.

2. Create Your Personal Mantra: Develop a powerful personal mantra that embodies your world-class self.

3. Start Your Morning Power Hour: Implement the Morning Power Hour routine for the next week.

4. Begin Your Victory Log: Start logging your daily victories, no matter how small.

5. Practice Emotional Intelligence: Use the emotion wheel to identify and name your feelings each day.

6. Implement the Integrity Check: At the end of each day, review whether your actions aligned with your values.

7. Develop Your Stress Resilience Routine: Create and practice your go-to routine for managing stress.

8. Find Your Accountability Partner: Reach out to someone who can

be your world-class accountability partner.

9. Start Your Skill Stack: Choose one new skill to start learning that will support your recovery.

10. Create Your Inspiration Bank: Collect quotes, stories, or images that inspire you to be world-class.

Conclusion: The World-Class Gladiator

Remember, Gladiators, this journey to world-class recovery isn't about perfection. It's about progress. It's about showing up every day and being committed to being the best version of yourself. It's about making amends not just through words but through consistent, excellent actions.

You're not just staying sober. You're becoming a world-class human being. You're becoming someone who inspires others and who makes a positive impact on the world just by being who you are.

This journey isn't always going to be easy. There will be days when you feel anything but world-class. But that's okay. What matters is that you keep showing up, trying and pushing to improve.

You've got this, Gladiators. You're stronger than you know, more resilient than you believe, and more world-class than you can imagine. Now, go out there and show the world what a truly world-class recovery looks like.

Round 10 is coming, and it's going to take everything you've got. But you're ready. You're world-class. Let's do this.

Round 10: Self-Reflection and Growth

(OR HOW TO STOP BULLSHITTING YOURSELF AND OWN YOUR SHIT)

ALRIGHT, GLADIATORS. WE'RE IN the tenth round of this fight. Welcome to Round 10: Self-Reflection and Growth. Our core value for this round? Don't make excuses.

Now, I know what you're thinking. "Ken, what the fuck? Isn't that a bit harsh?" Maybe. But you know what's harsher? Living a life where you constantly blame everything and everyone else for your problems. That's not freedom; that's a prison of your own making.

The Blame Game

In AA, Step 10 is about taking personal inventory and promptly admitting mistakes. Recovery Dharma talks about self-awareness. But we're going to take it a step further. We're going to assume that everything is our fault.

Let me break it down for you with a boxing analogy. In the ring, if you get punched in the face, it's your fault. You didn't slip, you didn't roll, you didn't block, you didn't parry. There's something you didn't do that got you clocked. And you know what? The same principle applies to life.

I remember this one fight I had early in my boxing training. I was feeling cocky, thought I had this guy figured out. Halfway through the second round, he landed a massive uppercut that I never saw coming and knocked me on my ass.

Now, I could've blamed my trainer for not preparing me properly. I could've blamed the coach for not calling some of this guy's borderline low blows. Hell, I could've blamed the fucking lighting in the gym for messing with my depth perception. But you know what? None of that would've changed the fact that I got hit.

It was my fault. I dropped my guard. I got overconfident. I wasn't paying attention. And once I accepted that I could learn from it. I could get better.

The same goes for our addiction and recovery. It's easy to blame the booze, our upbringing, our shitty boss, or whatever. But at the end of the day, we're the ones who picked up that bottle. Every. Single. Time.

The Accountability Revolution

Here's where it gets tricky. When you first get sober, it's tempting to keep blaming the alcohol. I used to have this phrase: "You can't blame sober Kenny for things that drunk Kenny did." It's a bullshit mindset, and I'm calling myself out on it right here and now.

Because at the end of the day, you are responsible for you. Drunk you, sober you, hungover you - it's all you. And the people in your life? They don't see drunk you and sober you as separate entities. They just see you.

I had to learn this the hard way. About a year into my sobriety, I ran into an old drinking buddy at the grocery store. This guy, let's call him Mike, he'd been on the receiving end of some of my drunken bullshit back in the day. I'd borrowed money I never paid back, stood him up more times than I could count, and even hit on his girlfriend once at a party.

So there I am, sober as a judge, feeling pretty good about myself. And I see Mike. I figure, hey, I'm sober now. Water under the bridge, right? Wrong. Mike took one look at me and walked the other way. And you know what? I don't blame him.

See, in my mind, I'd separated Drunk Kenny from Sober Kenny. But to Mike? I was just Kenny. The guy who'd been a shitty friend. The guy who'd hurt him. And no amount of sobriety was going to magically erase that.

That was a wake-up call. I realized that I couldn't just write off everything I'd done while drinking as "not the real me." It was all me. And I had to take responsibility for it if I wanted to truly change.

The Power of "It's My Fault"

Now, I'm not saying that literally, everything in the world is your fault. There are things beyond your control. Natural disasters, other people's actions, the fact that they canceled your favorite TV show - that shit isn't on you.

But most of the time, in most situations, there's something you could have done differently. And that's where the power lies. Because if it's your fault, that means you have the power to change it.

Take a DUI, for example. The obvious answer is, "I shouldn't have been drinking." But let's dig deeper. What if you had called a friend before you started drinking? What if you had planned for a ride home? What if you had chosen a different place to drink, one within walking distance of your house?

I knew this guy in one of my support groups; we'll call him Tom. Tom had three DUIs on his record. Every time, he had an excuse. The first time, it was his girlfriend's fault for breaking up with him. The second time, it was his boss's fault for stressing him out. The third time? He blamed the bartender for over-serving him.

Tom was stuck in a cycle. He never saw his part in it, so he never changed his behavior. It wasn't until his fourth DUI, when he finally ran out of people to blame, that he started to take responsibility. And you know what? That's when his real recovery began.

When you start thinking this way, you start seeing options you never saw before. You start taking control of your life in a whole new way.

The Art of "No Excuses"

Let's talk about excuses for a minute. Nobody wants to hear them. Your boss doesn't give a shit why you're late. Your partner doesn't care why you forgot to pick up milk. What they care about is what you're going to do about it.

So, instead of coming up with elaborate explanations, keep it simple. "I'm sorry I was late. It won't happen again." "I forgot the milk. I'll go get it now." Simple. Direct. No bullshit. And most importantly, it shows that you're taking responsibility and action.

I knew this woman in recovery; let's call her Sarah. Sarah was the queen of excuses. She always had a reason why she couldn't make meetings, missed a check-in with her sponsor, or had a slip.

One day, her sponsor called her out on it. Told her to go a whole week without making a single excuse. Just own her shit, whatever happened.

The first few days were rough. Sarah felt naked, exposed. But by the end of the week, something had changed. She felt lighter. She didn't have to keep track of all her lies and excuses. She could just be honest, deal with the consequences, and move on.

That week changed Sarah's life. She became one of the most reliable, accountable people in our group. All because she learned to stop making excuses.

Boundaries and Grace

Now, here's where it gets a bit tricky. When you start living this "no excuses" life, you will find that you need to set some boundaries. In our drinking days, boundaries were about as solid as a wet paper bag. Three beers in, and suddenly, you're everyone's best friend and willing to do anything for anyone.

Sober you? Sober you need boundaries. But here's the thing - as you set these new boundaries, you must practice a little grace. Not for yourself but for the people in your life who are used to the old you.

See, if you suddenly go from being the "yes man" to Mr. or Ms. Boundaries, you'll ruffle some feathers. People aren't going to understand what's happening. So, while you shouldn't make excuses for your boundaries, you might need to explain them. And give people a little time to adjust.

I learned this the hard way with my drinking buddies. When I first got sober, I cut them all off cold turkey. No explanation, no nothing. I was so focused on my sobriety that I didn't think about how it would affect them.

Months later, I ran into one of them at a coffee shop. He looked at me like I was a ghost. "We thought you were dead, man," he said. "You just disappeared."

That hit me hard. I realized that by trying to protect myself, I'd hurt people who cared about me. I hadn't given them a chance to understand or support my new lifestyle.

After that, I started reaching out. I explained my sobriety and set clear boundaries, but I also left the door open for those who wanted to be part of my new life. Some didn't get it, and that's okay. But others? They became my biggest supporters.

The Balancing Act

Let me give you another example. Let's say in your drinking days, you were always the one who drove everyone home from the bar. Now that you're sober, you've decided you're not going to hang out in bars anymore. That's a good boundary.

But if you just suddenly stop showing up without explanation, your friends might feel abandoned. They might not understand. So, you explain your boundary. You tell them why you're not coming to the bar anymore. You suggest alternative hangout spots. You give them time to adjust to this new you.

That's the balance between "no excuses" and grace. You're not making excuses for your boundary but giving others the grace to adapt to it.

I had a sponsee once; let's call him Dave. Dave was a people-pleaser in his drinking days. He'd agree to anything just to keep the peace. In early sobriety, he swung to the other extreme. He started saying no to everything and everyone without explanation.

His family was confused. His friends were hurt. His boss was pissed. Dave thought he was doing the right thing by setting boundaries, but he was doing it in a way that was alienating everyone around him.

We worked together on finding that balance. He learned to explain his boundaries, to offer alternatives when possible, and to be patient as people adjusted to the new Dave. It wasn't easy, but over time, his relationships improved. People respected his boundaries because they understood them.

The No-Excuses Mindset in Action

Living a life without excuses isn't easy. You're going to face some challenges. There will be times when you want to slip back into old patterns of blaming and excuse-making. Resist that urge.

It can be overwhelming when you start seeing how much of your life you actually control. Remember, you don't have to fix everything at once—one step at a time.

Some people in your life might not like this new, accountable you. They might try to push you back into old patterns. Stand firm.

There will be times when you wonder if you're being too hard on yourself. Remember, this isn't about beating yourself up. It's about empowering yourself to create change.

Don't confuse "no excuses" with "no mistakes." You're still going to fuck up sometimes. The key is how you handle it.

I remember when I was about two years sober, I got into a heated argument with my wife. In the heat of the moment, I said some things I regretted. Old me would have blamed it on stress, fatigue, or her for "pushing my buttons."

But new me? I took a deep breath, looked her in the eye, and said, "I'm sorry. What I said was hurtful and wrong. It won't happen again." And then, I got to work on managing my anger better. I started meditating, went to therapy, and learned better communication skills.

It wasn't about never getting angry again. It was about taking responsibility for how I expressed that anger.

The Ripple Effect of Responsibility

Here's something beautiful about this no-excuses approach to life: it doesn't just change you. It changes everything and everyone around you.

When you start taking full responsibility for your life, you inspire others. Your kids see what real accountability looks like. Your partner experiences what true commitment feels like. Your colleagues witness what genuine professionalism is.

This is how you grow. Not by pointing fingers but by pointing them at yourself and saying, "I can do better."

I saw this play out with a guy in one of my support groups. We'll call him John. John was a tough nut to crack. Always had an excuse, always had someone to blame. His wife was leaving him, his kids wouldn't talk to him, and he was on thin ice at work.

But slowly, session by session, John started to get it. He started owning his shit. And you know what? His life started to turn around. His wife saw the change and agreed to couples counseling. His kids started to trust him again. His boss noticed his improved performance and gave him more responsibilities.

John's transformation inspired others in the group. People who had been stuck in their own cycles of blame and excuses started to shift their perspectives. It was like watching a row of dominoes fall, one person's growth triggering another's.

The Gladiator's Guide to No Excuses

Alright, Gladiators, I know this "no excuses" thing can seem daunting. So here's a quick guide to help you put it into practice:

Catch yourself in the act. When something goes wrong, notice your first instinct. Is it to blame someone or something else?

Ask yourself, "What's my part in this?" There's always something, even if it's small.

Take action to make it right. Apologize if necessary, and devise a plan to do better next time.

Learn from it. Every mistake is an opportunity to grow.

Be patient with yourself. This is a process. You're rewiring years of habits.

Extend grace to others as they adjust to the new you.

Celebrate your wins. Taking responsibility is hard work. Acknowledge your progress.

Remember, this isn't about being perfect. It's about being accountable.

Conclusion: The No-Excuses Gladiator

Remember, Gladiators, this journey to a no-excuses life isn't about perfection. It's about progress. It's about showing up every day and being committed to taking full responsibility for your life and your recovery.

You're not just staying sober. You're becoming a person of integrity, a person who owns their shit and makes things happen. You're becoming someone who inspires others and who makes a positive impact on the world just by being who you are.

This journey isn't always going to be easy. There will be days when you want nothing more than to blame someone else, make an excuse, or take the easy way out. But that's okay. What matters is that you keep showing up, taking responsibility, and pushing to improve.

You've got this, Gladiators. You're stronger than you know, more resilient than you believe, and more capable than you can imagine. Now go out there and show the world what a truly no-excuses recovery looks like.

Round 11 is coming, and it's going to take everything you've got. But you're ready. You're a no-excuses Gladiator. Let's fucking do this.

Round 11: Spiritual Connection and Meaning

(OR HOW TO FIND YOUR COSMIC MOJO IN SOBRIETY)

ALRIGHT, GLADIATORS. WE'RE IN the eleventh round of this fight, and it's time to get metaphysical. Welcome to Round 11: Spiritual Connection and Meaning. Our core value for this round? Imagine. We're about to dive into the deep end of the spiritual pool, so take a deep breath and trust the process.

Now, I know what some of you are thinking. "Ken, what the fuck? I came here to get sober, not join a cult." Relax, warrior. We're not here to push any particular belief system on you. This is about finding what works for you, about tapping into something bigger than yourself to fuel your recovery journey.

The God Dilemma

Let me tell you a story. When I was a kid, maybe five, six, or seven years old, I used to lay in bed crying, wondering why nobody wanted me. I'd never met my biological father, my mom was wrestling with her own demons of addiction and PTSD, and I had a revolving door of step-siblings who were sometimes abusive, sometimes protective, and often absent.

I remember many nights begging that if there was a God, He'd take me out of this existence. And you know what? He never did. For a long time, that pushed me deep into atheism. I mean, how could there be a God if He'd put a kid through all this pain and confusion?

I was convinced that life itself was some kind of cosmic punishment. And let me tell you, that's a hell of a mindset to carry around. It's like trying to climb a mountain with a boulder strapped to your back.

The Unexplainable Experience

But here's where it gets weird. When I was about seven or eight, something happened that I couldn't explain for decades. I was lying in bed one night, and my stepdad and stepbrother were arguing in the kitchen. Pretty mellow night by our standards. And suddenly, I saw this bright light, like a lens flare, and I started crying hysterically. I had no idea what was happening.

Fast forward to my 40s. I'm 47, on a trip, working on the first version of this book. I'm still playing that moderation game with alcohol, thinking I've got it under control. Spoiler alert: I didn't.

During this trip, I was doing EMDR therapy, meditating, and trying to connect with nature. One night, during a meditation session, I traveled back to that night from my childhood. I saw myself as that little boy, and I told him everything would be okay.

In that moment, everything changed. It was like the universe cracked open and showed me a glimpse of something I can't even begin to explain.

The Cosmic Connection

Now, I'm not here to tell you I saw God or met aliens or anything like that. What I am saying is that there's more to this universe than what we can see and touch. Taping into that, whatever it is for you, can be a powerful tool in your recovery.

For me, it led me to pantheism - the idea that whatever you hold to be true will be true for you. It's that "as above, so below" kind of thinking. I've never believed in a single creator or subscribed to any one religion. But that experience opened me up to something bigger than myself.

And let me tell you, Gladiators, when you're fighting addiction, having something bigger than yourself to lean on? That's fucking powerful.

The Mindfulness Mindfuck

Here's the thing about spiritual experiences and mindfulness - they don't mix well with booze. When I was still playing that moderation game, I'd have these profound experiences, these moments of clarity and connection. And then I'd drink, and it all went out the window.

It's like building this beautiful sandcastle of awareness and then letting the tide of alcohol wash it all away. You go mindless. And it's not just when you're actively drinking. It's the hours and days around it, too.

I learned this the hard way on that same trip where I had my big spiritual breakthrough. Days after that experience, I was driving home through Georgia, not paying attention, and I got pulled over for speeding. One thing led to another, and I ended up illegally searched, arrested, strip-searched, and thrown in jail.

Talk about a cosmic bitchslap. One minute I was connecting with the universe, the next, I was walking down a jail corridor holding a mattress, trying not to get my ass kicked.

The Turning Point

But here's where it gets interesting. When I got out of jail that night, I bought a couple of tall boys. I figured, hey, I deserve a drink after the day I've had, right?

Wrong. I took two sips and couldn't stomach it. It wasn't who I was anymore. I didn't need to hurt myself or escape any longer. I knew who I was, and I knew that everything would be okay.

That, Gladiators, is the power of spiritual connection in recovery. It's not about finding God or becoming a monk or anything like that. It's about connecting with something bigger than yourself, something that gives you strength when your own reserves run dry.

The Meditation Station

Now, let's talk practical for a minute. How do you tap into this cosmic mojo? One word: meditation. And hear me out before you roll your eyes and tell me you can't sit still for five seconds.

Meditation isn't about emptying your mind or achieving a perfect zen state. It's about observing your thoughts and getting to know your own mind. And let me tell you, when you're in recovery, getting to know your mind is crucial.

Start small. Five minutes a day. Just sit, breathe, and watch your thoughts go by like clouds in the sky. Don't judge them; don't try to stop them. Just observe.

As you get more comfortable, you can try different techniques. Personally, I like to go to what I call "the bulk" - pure blackness, nothing around me. It's a place I've been able to reach since I was a kid.

Fair warning: this shit can get intense. My heart rate drops to about 42 beats per minute when I meditate like that. It feels like I'm on the edge of leaving this world. It's scary as hell, but it's also incredibly powerful.

The Imagination Station

Now, let's talk about our core value for this round: Imagine. This is where shit gets fun.

Imagination isn't just for kids or artists. It's a powerful tool in recovery. When you can imagine a better life for yourself and visualize yourself strong and sober, you're halfway there.

I've used imagination in my meditations to visit what I believe might be past lives. I've been a Neanderthal, an elephant, even a salmon. Now, am I saying I was literally these things in past lives? Who the fuck knows. I am saying that these experiences gave me perspective and helped me see my current struggles in a new light.

The Trust Fall

Here's the thing about spiritual connection and imagination - they require trust. Trust in yourself, the process, and maybe a higher power if that's your thing.

This isn't easy, especially for us addicts. We've spent years betraying our trust, letting ourselves down repeatedly. But recovery is about rebuilding that trust with ourselves and the universe.

Start small. Trust that you can make it through today sober. Trust that the cravings will pass. Trust that you're on the right path, even when it feels like you're lost in the woods.

As you build that trust, you'll find it easier to tap into that spiritual connection, to let your imagination guide you towards a better future.

The Gladiator's Guide to Spiritual Connection

Alright, Gladiators, I know this spiritual stuff can seem overwhelming. So here's a quick guide to help you get started:

1. Start daily meditation practice. Even 5 minutes a day can make a difference.

2. Keep a spiritual journal. Write down your experiences, your questions, and your insights.

3. Explore different spiritual practices. Find what resonates with you.

4. Practice gratitude. Feeling spiritually connected is hard when you're focused on the negative.

5. Spend time in nature. There's something about the natural world that puts things in perspective.

6. Use your imagination. Visualize your ideal sober life. Imagine yourself strong and centered.

7. Trust the process. Recovery is a journey, not a destination.

Remember, this isn't about finding the "right" way to be spiritual. It's about finding what works for you.

Conclusion: The Spiritually Connected Gladiator

Remember, Gladiators, this journey to spiritual connection isn't about becoming some enlightened guru. It's about finding meaning in your life beyond the bottle. It's about tapping into something bigger than yourself to fuel your recovery.

You're not just staying sober. You're becoming a person connected to something greater, a person who can imagine and create a better future. You're becoming someone who trusts in the process of recovery and in their own inner strength.

This journey isn't always going to be easy. There will be days when you feel disconnected, and the universe seems cold and uncaring. But that's okay. What matters is that you keep showing up, keep exploring, and keep imagining.

You've got this, Gladiators. You're stronger than you know, more connected than you realize, and more imaginative than you can... well, imagine. Now, go out there and show the world what a truly spiritually connected recovery looks like.

Round 12 is coming, and it will take everything you've got. But you're ready. You're a spiritually connected, imaginative Gladiator. Let's fucking do this.

Round 12: Sharing the Journey

(OR HOW TO BE A SOBER BADASS AND LIGHT THE WAY FOR OTHERS)

ALRIGHT, GLADIATORS. WE'VE MADE it to the final round. Round 12: Sharing the Journey. Our core value for this round? Imagination and belief. Because let me tell you, the way you see yourself and the future you envision? That shit matters more than you know.

The Misfit's Journey

Let's start with a truth bomb: I've never felt like I fit in. Not really. Sure, when I was drinking at the bar and having a good time, it felt like I belonged. But that was just the booze talking. Even now, stone-cold sober, I still feel like an individual that's part of something different, something else.

And you know what? That's okay. It's more than okay. It's fucking powerful.

For the longest time, I thought something was wrong with me because I couldn't find my tribe. But here's the thing: sometimes you don't find your tribe. Sometimes you have to create it.

The Community Conundrum

Now, let's talk about community. Being part of a community has been one of the biggest tools in my recovery toolkit. But here's the kicker: it doesn't work all the time or for everyone. You have to be in the right spot for it.

Let me take you on a little journey through my attempts at finding community. At 13 years old, I got arrested for Grand Theft Auto, possession of marijuana (over a pound), curfew violation, possession of alcohol, and being drunk. Yeah, I was an overachiever in all the wrong ways.

After that, I went through a program in the 80s called "Tough Love." Let me tell you, it was a far cry from how we treat our youth today. That was my first time in youth AA and my first time in group counseling. Did it work? Hell no. I didn't want to be there and didn't try to connect. I was too good for it, or so I thought.

Throughout my life, I tried other rehab programs, different types of therapy, and even hypnosis. I tried nearly anything you can think of, except for those drugs that make you sick when you drink. I never tried those because when I was a kid, they put me on Wellbutrin to get me to quit smoking. I'd just smoke anyway, and it would taste like shit. I'd lean off the medicine and keep right on puffing.

The Tool Box Approach

Here's what I learned from all that: there are a lot of tools out there, and no one tool is the solution. Part of the goal of this book is to supply you with a variety of tools and slight variations on a theme so that you can build your own recipe for sobriety.

It's like being a master chef. You don't just use one ingredient or one cooking method for every dish. You mix and match, you experiment, and you find what works for you. And sometimes, you have to invent your own dishes.

The Belief Barrier

Now, let's talk about belief. This shit is powerful, more powerful than you might realize. Alcoholics Anonymous does a great job of getting people to stop drinking. What they don't do so well is keeping people from relapsing. You've got to find something different most of the time.

See, when you're in active addiction, you don't think you're an alcoholic. You think everything's fine, or at least most people do. That's denial for you. So you have to believe you're an alcoholic before you can get help. That's how powerful belief is.

But here's where it gets tricky. I always knew I was an alcoholic. It was who I identified as, part of who I was, part of what made me a man. Men get drunk, they drink whiskey, they drink beer, they ride motorcycles, and they get women. That's what I always believed, what I was always taught.

And that belief? It let me relapse on any occasion that came around. Because that's what alcoholics do, right? They relapse. It's part of the deal.

The Identity Shift

I had to change my belief structure. I had to believe that I was a sober man, not an alcoholic. And let me tell you, there are no fucking programs for that. So, I had to create my own stuff. And that's okay.

This is where SMART Recovery came in for me. It's the closest I've found to what I needed. I'm a certified SMART Recovery practitioner now, and I try to attend a meeting every week. It's part of my community and how I fit in and belong.

Don't get me wrong, it's a fucked-up group. But they're all great people, and it's nice to see others who have the same struggles as you or similar struggles achieving good things in life. Seeing other people do it is part of what helps me believe that I can do it.

The Power of Identification

Here's something I believe with every fiber of my being: if you walk out into the world with the mindset that you are an addict, there are situations that can occur that would put you into a relapse scenario. But if you walk out the door and identify as a sober human, man or woman, there are not too many reasons that you would relapse because drinking is just something that you don't do anymore.

So, if you're stuck in this mindset of "My name is Ken, and I'm an alcoholic," I challenge you to try this: "Hi, my name is Ken, and I'm a sober person." If you're not comfortable with that yet, try "Hi, my name is Ken, and I'm sober today, and I plan on being sober tomorrow."

Even if you don't believe it today, saying it will change your life. You have to be consistent with it. Sometimes you even have to practice, just like that "I love and respect you" shit in the mirror.

The Ripple Effect

Now, let's talk about sharing this journey. When you start identifying as a sober person and living that sober life with pride and purpose, you become a beacon for others. You show them what's possible.

I remember the first time I turned down a drink at a work event, and someone asked me why. Instead of mumbling some excuse about antibiotics or driving, I looked them in the eye and said, "I'm a sober man. I don't drink." The look on their face was priceless. But more than that, later that night, a colleague approached me and said, "I've been thinking about quitting. Seeing you do it makes me think maybe I can too."

That, Gladiators, is the power of sharing your journey. You never know who's watching, who's struggling, who needs to see someone like them living a sober life.

The Challenges of Sharing

Now, I'm not going to bullshit you. Sharing your journey isn't always easy. There will be people who don't get it, try to push drinks on you, and tell you that you're no fun anymore. Fuck 'em. You're not doing this for them. You're doing it for you.

There will also be times when you feel like a fraud. Times when the cravings hit hard and you wonder who the hell you are to be advising anyone. That's normal. That's part of the process. The key is to keep showing up, being honest, and sharing your truth.

The Balance Act

One of the trickiest parts of sharing your journey is balancing helping others with maintaining your own sobriety. It's like they tell you on airplanes - put your own oxygen mask on first before helping others.

I learned this the hard way. Early in my recovery, I threw myself into helping others. I was sponsoring guys and speaking at meetings the whole nine yards. And you know what? I burned out. I got so focused on everyone else's recovery that I neglected my own.

Now, I make sure to take care of myself first. I have my non-negotiables - my meditation practice, my SMART Recovery meetings, and my time with my family. Only when those are taken care of will I extend myself to help others.

The Future of Recovery

Here's something I believe with every fiber of my being: the future of addiction recovery lies in empowerment, not in labeling ourselves as permanently broken. It lies in communities of sober badasses supporting each other, not in hierarchy and dogma.

Imagine a world where being sober isn't seen as a limitation but as a superpower. Where we're not "recovering addicts" but "evolved humans who've chosen a better way to live." That's the world I'm working towards, and I invite you to join me in creating it.

The Gladiator's Guide to Sharing the Journey

Alright, Gladiators, here's your guide to sharing your journey and lighting the way for others:

1. Own Your Story: Your journey is unique. Don't be ashamed of it. Own it, learn from it, share it.

2. Lead by Example: Living your journey fully is the most powerful way to share it. Be the sober badass you wish you'd seen when you were struggling.

3. Be Honest: Share your struggles as well as your victories. People need to know that recovery isn't always easy, but it's always worth it.

4. Respect Others' Journeys: What worked for you might not work for everyone. Share your experience, but don't preach.

5. Keep Learning: Stay open to new ideas and approaches. The more tools you have in your recovery toolkit, the more you can share with others.

6. Practice Self-Care: Remember, you can't pour from an empty cup. Take care of yourself first.

7. Use Your Imagination: Envision a better future for yourself and others struggling with addiction. Then, work to make it a reality.

8. Believe in the Possible: Believe in yourself, others, and the power

of recovery. Your belief can move mountains.

Conclusion: The Journey Continues

Remember, Gladiators, this journey doesn't end here. Recovery isn't a destination; it's a way of life. And by sharing your journey, you're not just helping others - you're reinforcing your own recovery, you're creating a community, you're changing the fucking world.

You're not just staying sober. You're becoming a beacon of hope, a source of inspiration, a goddamn superhero in the fight against addiction. You're showing the world that there's life after addiction, and it's fucking beautiful.

This journey isn't always going to be easy. There will be days when you question everything and wonder if you have anything worth sharing. But that's okay. What matters is that you keep showing up, being honest, and lighting the way for others.

You've got this, Gladiators. You're stronger than you know, more inspiring than you realize, and more capable of change than you can imagine. Now, go out there and show the world what a truly empowered, sober life looks like.

This is the end of our 12 rounds, but it's just the beginning of your journey as a Sobriety Gladiator. Keep fighting the good fight. Keep sharing your truth. Keep believing in the power of sobriety.

You are worth the effort. Believe that you can get there. Because if one human on this planet can do it, so can you.

Now get out there and be the sober badass you were always meant to be. The world is waiting for you.

The Press Conference

(OR HOW TO FACE THE WORLD AS A SOBER BADASS)

ALRIGHT, GLADIATORS. YOU'VE GONE through all 12 rounds. You've fought hard, you've bled, you've stumbled, but you're still standing. Now it's time for the press conference. Time to face the world, reflect on your journey, and look to the future.

Now, I'm not going to bullshit you. This isn't some fairy tale ending where everything's perfect, and you ride off into the sunset. That's not how this works. You're still going to have to see your opponent. That anxiety might still show up when addiction rears its ugly head. But here's the difference - you don't have to fight anymore. You're not in the ring. You're at the podium, and you're in control.

Let me tell you something about those first months of recovery. You might have heard people talk about the "pink cloud" - this euphoric state where you feel you can conquer the world. Well, I never got that. Not once. Instead, I was angry. Fucking pissed, to be honest.

I was mad that I couldn't do what I wanted to do and handle it. I'd make bullshit statements like, "I never had a problem with alcohol. Other people have a problem with me and alcohol." I'm talking about my wife and the doctors. With that attitude, it was no wonder I had such a problem not drinking.

It was a challenge just to drive the 6 miles from my office to my home. I passed two gas stations on that route and would tremble driving past them. I wanted so badly to pull in and grab a beer or two on my way home, just like I used to do regularly. But I couldn't anymore, and it was killing me.

That anger reduced over time, but it was always there, lurking in the background until I changed my mindset - until I had the battle, won, and walked away. Now, I'm not in this fight with addiction anymore. I'm a sober man. That's who I am, and I can say it proudly and with confidence.

Here's something I've learned from coaching people - both addicts and non-addicts. There's power in identity, whether it's helping someone overcome addiction, coaching young boxers to overcome their fear and step into the ring, or guiding small businesses to build their online presence.

I'm not hundred percent sure which is more powerful - identifying as something you want to be or refusing to identify as something you don't want to be. But I do know this: anyone I've ever coached who stands proudly and knows who they are is a powerful person.

Dealing with the negative keeps you in a depressed state. It won't do you any good. You can lose a fight as a sober person and still stand at the press conference with pride and say, "I screwed up. I should have done X, Y, Z. These are the things I will do to make sure it doesn't happen again."

But when I identified as an addict? A slip, a three-day bender, a 10-day relapse, or even a 2-year relapse was just par for the course. Because I was an addict, and that's what addicts do. I had that built-in excuse.

The first time I really committed to trying to stop drinking was when I was 40 years old, 9 years ago, as I wrote this book. I still tried the moderation game from time to time. I strung together a couple of good years here and there. But it wasn't until I changed my mindset and changed who I was that everything changed for me.

Now, here's the bitch of it all. Even if you win this fight - and I know you will if you keep trying - you're going to walk away with some bumps and bruises. Your loved ones might think that all the problems should be fixed because alcohol was the problem. But you've got a lot of work to do.

You've learned a lot to quit. You've learned a lot to change your mind to be sober. But there's still a lot of work ahead of you. You've burned a lot of fields. That's okay. Do your best moving forward. Be a better person - not better than anybody else, just a better person than you were yesterday.

There are a couple of worksheets in the back of this book. If you want to use them, use them. I find some of them helpful. We'll do them all together if you join me in a group bootcamp. But here's a reminder: we did a lot of lists and homework in this book. Do the ones that come naturally to you. Ignore the others. If something feels particularly uncomfortable, I suggest leaning into that one. There's probably a reason it's uncomfortable.

Love yourself. You're important. You deserve it. There is suffering in this world, but there is also an end to suffering. All things on this beautiful planet are possible. You've got this.

I chose the Gladiator metaphor for so many reasons. Gladiators were generally slaves, as we were to alcohol. They fought for other people's entertainment; we fight for ourselves. But I promise you, people are watching. Some of those people want us to succeed. Some of those people want us to fail. Hopefully, those who want you to succeed are your spouse, children, close co-workers, and close friends.

I don't believe you can be the best version of yourself if you drink alcohol every day of your life. When you're the best version of yourself, you're going to help other people. You're going to help build them up. You're going to practice what you've learned.

If only one person reads any line of this book and it gets them one day closer to sobriety, it's worth all the time and effort I've put into sharing these details.

So here you are, Gladiator, at the press conference of your life. The reporters are clamoring, and the cameras are flashing. What are you going to say?

Are you going to talk about your struggles, your setbacks? Sure, be honest about them. But don't dwell on them. Instead, talk about your victories. Talk about the person you've become. Talk about the life you're building.

When they ask you about your opponent, about addiction, don't give it more power than it deserves. You respect its strength, sure. But you're not afraid of it anymore. You're not its victim. You're not even its opponent anymore. You're just you - a sober, badass version of you.

And when they ask you what's next? Tell them the truth. Tell them you're going to keep growing and keep improving. Tell them you'll help others find their way out of the arena. Tell them you're going to live a life so fucking amazing that it makes your old drinking days look like the sad, pathetic charade they were.

Remember, Gladiator, this press conference isn't the end. It's just the beginning of a new chapter. You're going to face challenges. You're going to have days when you question everything. But you've got the tools now. You've got the mindset. You've got the strength.

You're not just sober. You're not just recovering. You're thriving. You're a fucking Sobriety Gladiator.

So go out there and show the world what that means. Live your life with pride, with purpose, with passion. Be the inspiration that someone else needs to make the change in their life.

And always remember: You've got this. You're worth it. And the best is yet to come.

Now, go out there and conquer the world, one sober day at a time.

WORKSHEETS

Hierarchy of Values

A GLADIATOR'S GUIDE TO PRIORITIES

ALRIGHT, GLADIATORS. IT'S TIME to get real about what matters in your life. This Hierarchy of Values exercise isn't just some feel-good bullshit. It's a powerful tool to help you align your actions with what you truly care about.

Here's how it works:

1. Take a few minutes to list everything that's important to you. Don't hold back. This is your life we're talking about.

2. Now, the hard part. Choose the top five things from that list. These are your non-negotiables, the things you'd fight for in the arena of life.

3. Write these five things in the space provided below.

Now, here's where it gets interesting. Look at your list. Is alcohol on there? Drugs? Probably not. Yet how many times have you put that poison above everything else on your list?

Every time you choose to drink or use, you're saying that your addiction is more important than the five things you just wrote down. You're throwing your gladiator shield away and leaving yourself exposed to the enemy.

But here's the good news: You're a fucking Gladiator now. You have the power to flip the script.

Imagine "Sobriety" at the top of that list. When you prioritize your sobriety, you're automatically protecting everything else on that list. It's like the ultimate shield, guarding all that you hold dear.

Use this worksheet as a reminder of what you're fighting for. When the cravings hit, when you're tempted to fall back into old habits, pull this out. Remember what's truly important.

This isn't just about not drinking or using. It's about becoming the person who values these five things more than anything else. It's about being the Gladiator who fights for what matters, not the slave who surrenders to addiction.

So, Gladiator, what are your top five? What are you willing to step into the arena for? Write them down, commit them to memory, and let them fuel your fight for sobriety.

Remember: You're not just staying sober. You're reclaiming your life, one value at a time. Now get out there and show addiction who's boss.

My Top 5 Values: Use this space to Write down your Top 5 Core Values.

Hierarchy of Values

A GLADIATOR'S GUIDE TO PRIORITIES

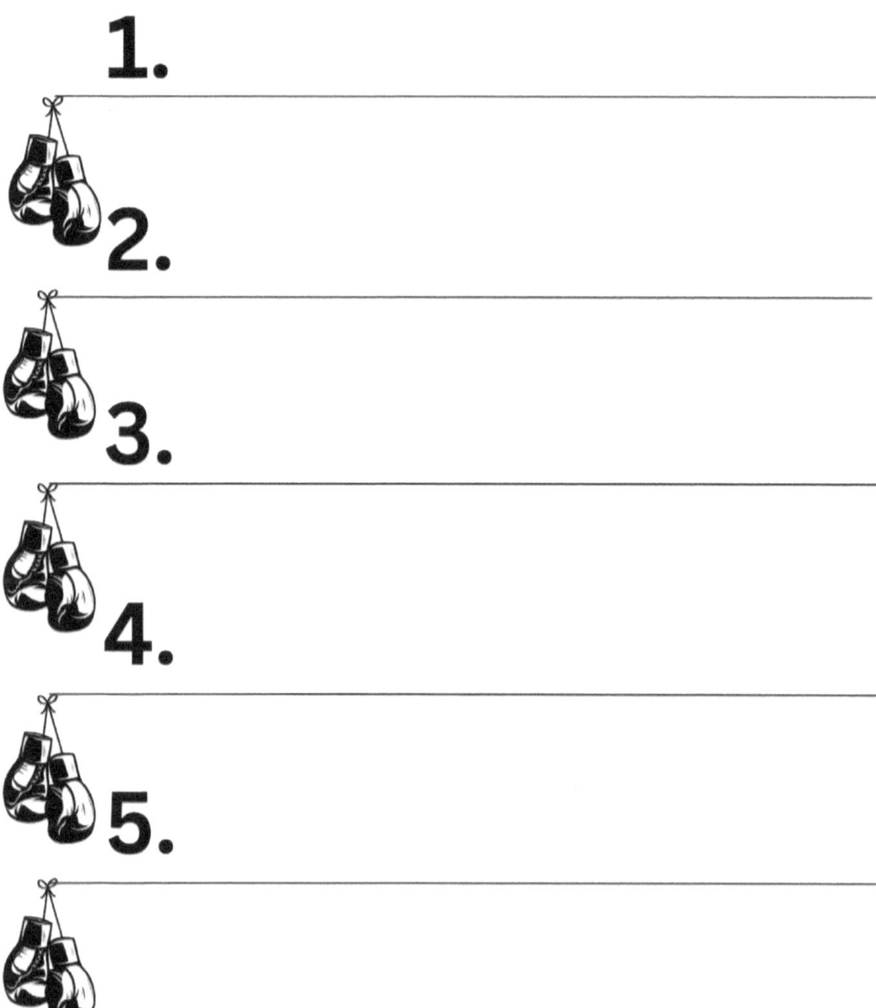

1. ____

2. ____

3. ____

4. ____

5. ____

CHANGE-PLAN Worksheet

A GLADIATOR'S BATTLE STRATEGY

LISTEN UP, GLADIATOR. YOU'RE about to enter the arena of change, and you need a battle plan. This isn't some fluffy self-help exercise – this is your strategy for conquering addiction and reclaiming your life.

Just like a seasoned warrior doesn't charge into battle without a plan, you're not going to tackle this fight without a solid strategy. This worksheet is your war room, where you'll map out your attack, identify your allies, and prepare for the obstacles ahead.

Remember, in the arena of recovery, clarity is your weapon and determination is your shield. So let's sharpen that focus and steel that resolve. It's time to plan your victory.

How to Wield This Weapon:

Changes I Want to Make: These are your targets. Be specific. "Stop drinking" is a start, but "Replace my 6 PM beer with a gym session" is a battle cry.

Importance and Confidence Scales: Rate these from 1-10. This isn't just number crunching – it's about honest self-assessment. If your importance is high but confidence is low, you know where you need to build strength.

Most Important Reasons: This is your "why". When the battle gets tough, these reasons will be the war cry that keeps you fighting.

Steps to Take: Break down your strategy. Every great victory is won through a series of smaller battles.

How Others Can Help: Even the mightiest gladiator needs allies. Identify your support squad and how they can have your back.

Knowing the Plan is Working: Define your victories. How will you know you're winning this war?

Potential Interferences: Scout your enemy. What obstacles might you face? Forewarned is forearmed, Gladiator.

Now, grab your metaphorical sword and let's start planning your road to victory. Remember, in this arena, you're not fighting against others – you're fighting for yourself. Every plan you make, every step you take, is another blow against addiction and another stride towards the freedom you deserve.

Are you ready, Gladiator? Let's do this.

What changes do I Want to Make:

On a Scale of 1 - 10 how confident am I that I can make this change?:

What is my most important reason, Why or Who am I making this change for?:

What steps am i commenting to take to make this change happen for me?:

Who is in my Corner to help me out?:

What will Success Look like?:

What can fuck this up?:

Gladiator's Cost-Benefit Analysis

In your journey to reclaim sobriety, understanding the true costs and benefits of your behaviors is crucial. This Gladiator's Cost-Benefit Analysis (CBA) worksheet is designed to help you gain clarity and reinforce your commitment to making positive changes. By weighing the short-term and long-term consequences of your actions, you can make more informed decisions that align with your values and goals.

How to Use This Worksheet:

1. Identify the Behavior:

- Start by identifying the specific behavior you want to analyze. This could be anything related to your sobriety journey, such as the decision to drink, use substances, or engage in any other addictive behavior. Alternatively, you can use this worksheet to analyze a positive behavior you're considering adopting, like attending a support group or starting a new hobby.

2. Label Short-Term (ST) and Long-Term (LT) Effects:

- For each behavior, consider both the short-term and long-term effects. Label each item accordingly as you document the potential costs (risks and disadvantages) and benefits (rewards and advantages) of engaging in or avoiding the behavior.

- For example, the short-term benefit of drinking might be immediate stress relief, but the long-term cost could be the negative impact on your health, relationships, and overall progress in recovery.

3. Weigh the Costs and Benefits:

- Take a moment to reflect on the costs and benefits you've listed. How do the short-term rewards compare to the long-term consequences? Are the immediate benefits worth the potential setbacks? This step is about being honest with yourself and recognizing patterns that may be holding you back.

4. Evaluate Your Motivation:

- Use the insights gained from this analysis to reinforce your motivation for change. If you notice that the long-term costs outweigh the short-term benefits, this can serve as a powerful reminder of why it's important to stay committed to your recovery.

5. Plan Your Next Steps:

- Based on your analysis, decide on your next steps. If the costs of a behavior are too high, consider what changes you need to make. If the benefits of a positive behavior are significant, think about how you can incorporate more of that into your life.

Why This Worksheet Matters:

This worksheet is more than just an exercise—it's a tool to help you build the life you want. By taking the time to evaluate the true impact of your behaviors, you empower yourself to make decisions that support your long-term sobriety and well-being. Remember, every small decision adds up, and this analysis can guide you in making choices that align with the person you're becoming.

Your journey to reclaim sobriety is a series of deliberate choices. Use this Gladiator's Cost-Benefit Analysis to ensure those choices lead you to the life you deserve.

<table>
<tr><td colspan="2" align="center">Gladiator's Cost-Benefit Analysis</td></tr>
<tr><td colspan="2">Using_____________________________________or Doing________________________________</td></tr>
<tr><td>Short Term and Long Term Benefits
(Rewards and Advantages)</td><td>Short Term and Long Term Costs
(Risks and Disadvantages)</td></tr>
<tr><td>

</td><td></td></tr>
<tr><td colspan="2">Not Using_______________________________Or Doing________________________________</td></tr>
<tr><td>Short Term and Long Term Benefits
(Rewards and Advantages)</td><td>Short Term and Long Term Costs
(Risks and Disadvantages)</td></tr>
<tr><td>

</td><td></td></tr>
</table>

Gladiator's Reality Check

BELIEFS ABOUT URGES

IN YOUR JOURNEY TO reclaim sobriety, it's crucial to understand and challenge the beliefs you have about the urges you experience. This worksheet will help you break down those urges and replace unhelpful beliefs with empowering truths. Use this exercise to strengthen your mental resilience and stay on the path to victory.

How to Use This Worksheet:

1. Identify the Situation/Trigger:

- Start by describing the situation or trigger that led to your urge. What was happening around you? What were you feeling? Understanding the context is the first step in breaking the cycle.

2. Acknowledge the Urge:

- Write down the specific urge you experienced. What did you feel compelled to do? This could be an urge to drink, use substances, or engage in any other behavior that challenges your sobriety.

3. **Examine Your Belief:**

   ○ Reflect on the belief you had about the urge. Did you believe that giving in was the only way to cope? Did you feel powerless against it? Write down the thoughts that accompanied the urge.

4. **Challenge the Belief with Reality:**

   ○ Now, it's time to challenge that belief with a reality check. What is the truth of the situation? Is the urge really as powerful as it seems? What are the consequences of giving in versus resisting? Write down the reality of the situation and how your true strength can overcome the urge.

Situation/Trigger	Urge	Belief	Reality Check
Describe the situation that triggered the urge.	What urge did you experience?	What belief did you have about the urge?	What is the reality of the situation?

Gladiator's Battle Plan

CONQUERING URGES

IN YOUR FIGHT TO reclaim sobriety, every urge is a challenge that must be met with strength, strategy, and determination. The Gladiator's Battle Plan, also known as the DEADS method, provides you with a set of powerful tools to confront and overcome these urges. This plan will help you stay focused and resilient, ensuring that you remain victorious in your pursuit of a sober life.

How to Use the Gladiator's Battle Plan:

1 – D = Deny / Delay

- **Strategy:** Refuse to give in to the urge, no matter what. Deny its power over you and delay any action until the urge passes. Remind yourself that most urges last only 10-20 minutes. Stand firm in the knowledge that you have the strength to outlast it.

- **Reflection:** How long do your urges usually last if you don't give in? How intense do they become before they start to fade? What immediate actions can you take to help you deny them?

Write Your Strategy:

____

____

____

____

____

____

2 – E = Escape

- **Strategy:** Identify the triggers that spark your urges. Escape their influence by removing yourself from the situation as quickly as possible. Whether it's a place, person, or object, create distance between you and the trigger.

- **Reflection:** What triggers can you escape from? How can you remove yourself from their influence when an urge arises?

Write Your Strategy:

____

____

____

____

____

____

3 – A = Avoid, Accept, or Attack

- **Strategy:** Choose your approach—avoid known triggers, accept the urge and let it pass, or attack it with the tools you've learned. These are your weapons in the battle against temptation.

- **Reflection:** What can you do to avoid urges? How can you accept the urge without giving in? What tools or words will you use to attack the urge when it strikes?

Write Your Strategy:

____

____

____

____

____

____

4 – D = Distract Yourself with an Activity

- **Strategy:** When an urge arises, shift your focus by engaging in an activity that takes your mind off it. Distraction is a powerful tactic in the heat of battle—keep yourself busy and the urge will lose its grip.

- **Reflection:** What activities can you do to distract yourself? How can you fill the time that you used to spend on your addictive behavior?

Write Your Strategy:

____

____

____

____

____

____

5 – S = Substitute for Addictive Thinking

- **Strategy:** Replace harmful thoughts with empowering ones. Substitute destructive behaviors with positive, life-affirming activities. This is how you build resilience and fortify your defenses.

- **Reflection:** What thoughts have you developed to challenge the illogical thinking that comes with urges? What healthy activities can you do to replace negative thinking and feelings?

Write Your Strategy:

____

____

____

____

____

When to Use This Tool:

This Gladiator's Battle Plan is your guide to staying strong, no matter how intense the urge. Use it whenever you feel the pull of old habits. By consistently applying these strategies, you will build the mental and emotional armor needed to reclaim your sobriety and win the war against addiction.

Gladiator's Mind Armor

DISPUTING IRRATIONAL BELIEFS (DIBS)

IN THE HEAT OF battle, a Gladiator knows that the mind can be either their strongest weapon or their greatest weakness. Irrational beliefs are like cracks in your armor—they weaken you and make you vulnerable to the forces you're fighting against. The Gladiator's Mind Armor technique, also known as Disputing Irrational Beliefs (DIBs), is designed to help you identify these mental cracks and replace them with the strength of rational thinking. This exercise will fortify your mind, ensuring that you remain resilient and focused on your path to sobriety.

How to Use the Gladiator's Mind Armor:

1. **Identify Your Irrational Belief:**

   - Write down the irrational belief that is currently challenging your sobriety. These beliefs are often unrealistic, illogical, and harmful—they do not serve your long-term goals. Examples might include thoughts like "I can't handle this urge," or "I'll never be able to stop."

2. **Question the Irrational Belief:**

   - Challenge this belief by turning it into a question. Ask yourself:

Is this really true? Does it make sense? What evidence do I have to support or refute this belief? This step is about taking control and not letting irrational thoughts dictate your actions.

3. Formulate Your Rational Belief:

- After questioning the irrational belief, replace it with a rational belief that is true, logical, and helpful. For example, if your irrational belief is "I can't cope without using," your rational belief might be "I've coped before, and my life is better when I'm not using."

Example of Gladiator's Mind Armor in Action:

My Irrational Belief	Question My Irrational Belief	My Rational Belief
"Urges are unbearable and I cannot stand them."	"Are urges unbearable?"	"No, urges are unpleasant but they won't kill me. I can endure them, and they will pass."
"I'll just have one drink."	"Will I really just have one?"	"No, I never stop at one. If I start, I'll just get drunk again."
"I cannot cope without using."	"Can I cope without using?"	"Yes, I've coped before, and my life is better when I'm not using."

When to Use This Tool:

This Gladiator's Mind Armor technique is a powerful tool to use whenever you find yourself struggling with thoughts that challenge your sobriety. By consistently applying this method, you will strengthen your mental resilience and reinforce the rational beliefs that support your recovery.

Remember, a true Gladiator knows that victory begins in the mind—arm yourself with rational thinking, and no challenge will be too great.

My Irrational Belief	Question My Irrational Belief	My Rational Belief

Gladiator's Language of Strength

CHANGING YOUR VOCABULARY, CHANGING YOUR FEELINGS

A GLADIATOR KNOWS THAT words hold power—both the words spoken aloud and those we say to ourselves. The way you talk to yourself can either weaken your resolve or fortify your strength. This worksheet, "Gladiator's Language of Strength," is designed to help you transform your internal dialogue, replacing words that make you feel powerless with those that empower you to continue your fight for sobriety.

How to Use the Gladiator's Language of Strength:

1. **Statement Exchange:**

   - Identify statements you commonly say to yourself that undermine your strength. These might be phrases like "I can't do this" or "I'm not strong enough."

   - For each negative statement, create a new, empowering one that reflects the true strength of a Gladiator. Replace "I can't do this" with "I have the strength to overcome this."

2. Emotion Vocabulary Exchange:

- Pay attention to the words you use to describe your emotions. Negative emotions are often intensified by the words we use to describe them. For example, instead of saying "I'm devastated," try "I'm challenged, but I will endure."

- Choose words that reflect resilience and determination. This small change in vocabulary can have a significant impact on how you feel and how you respond to challenges.

Example of Gladiator's Language in Action:

Negative Statement	Empowering Gladiator Statement	Negative Emotion Word	Empowering Emotion Word
"I can't handle this."	"I am strong enough to handle anything."	"Overwhelmed"	"Challenged"
"This is too hard."	"I will rise to the challenge."	"Devastated"	"Enduring"
"I'm not good enough."	"I have the power to succeed."	"Hopeless"	"Determined"
"I'll never change."	"I am constantly growing stronger."	"Anxious"	"Focused"
"I always fail."	"Every setback is a step toward success."	"Frustrated"	"Resilient"
"This is impossible."	"I will find a way through this."	"Defeated"	"Resolute"

When to Use This Tool:

This Gladiator's Language of Strength is your tool to reshape the way you think and feel about the challenges you face in sobriety. Use it whenever you catch yourself using disempowering language. By consistently applying this strategy, you'll strengthen your mental and emotional resilience, making you more capable of overcoming any obstacle on your path to reclaiming sobriety.

Remember, words are weapons—choose those that empower you and forge ahead with the strength of a true Gladiator.

Gladiator's Shield

THE LIFESTYLE BALANCE PIE

As a Gladiator on the path to reclaiming your life, balance is your shield—it protects you from the dangers of relapse and helps you maintain the strength needed to continue fighting for your sobriety. The Lifestyle Balance Pie is a powerful tool that helps you assess how well you're balancing the different aspects of your life, ensuring that you're living in a way that supports both your immediate recovery and your long-term well-being.

How to Use the Gladiator's Shield:

1. **Divide Your Life into Sections:**

   - Imagine your life as a pie, with each slice representing a different area of your life. Consider the following categories:

     - **Self-Maintenance:** The essential activities that keep you functioning, like work, cooking, and maintaining your living space.

     - **Self-Development:** The activities that challenge and grow you, such as learning new skills, engaging in hobbies, or pursuing personal goals.

     - **Fun:** The activities that bring you joy and relaxation, like spending time with family and friends, or enjoying your favorite leisure activities.

2. **Rate Your Satisfaction:**

- For each slice of your life pie, rate your current level of satisfaction on a scale from 0 to 10, with 10 being completely satisfied and 0 being totally dissatisfied. Place a dot on each slice corresponding to your satisfaction level.

- Connect the dots to see how balanced your life is. If your life pie looks full and round, you're maintaining a good balance. If there are dips and gaps, it may be a sign that some areas need more attention.

3. **Assess the Balance:**

- After completing your pie, take a step back and assess the overall balance of your life. Ask yourself:

  - Am I living a balanced life, or are there areas that need more focus?

  - Are my true values and priorities reflected in how I spend my time?

  - If I had one month left to live, would I be spending my time this way?

  - Am I overburdened with too many activities, or neglecting important areas of my life?

  - How much of my time is dedicated to caring for others versus caring for myself?

- What areas of my life could use more attention to help me feel more balanced?

4. Plan Your Next Moves:

- Identify which slices of your pie need more attention and what specific changes you can make to improve balance. Consider what activities you can add, reduce, or adjust to create a more even distribution of time and energy across all areas of your life.

Example of Gladiator's Shield in Action:

Life Category	Satisfaction Score (0-10)	Plan to Improve Balance
Self-Maintenance	6	Set aside time for meal planning and home maintenance.
Self-Development	4	Enroll in an online course or start a new hobby
Fun	7	Schedule regular social outings or relaxation time.

Why This Matters:

Balance is crucial to maintaining your strength and resilience as a Gladiator in the fight for sobriety. By regularly assessing and adjusting your lifestyle, you can ensure that you're living in a way that not only supports your recovery but also brings long-term satisfaction and fulfillment.

Remember, a well-balanced life is your best defense. Keep your shield strong and ready, and continue moving forward with confidence and purpose.

Today's Date:

Life Category	Satisfaction Score (0-10)	Plan to Improve Balance

Lowest Scores	
Life Category	Score
Highest Scores	
What is your Plan?	

Ready to take your journey to the next level?

Your purchase of "Reclaim Sobriety: 12 Rounds to Sobriety" is just the beginning. As a special gift to our dedicated Gladiators, we're offering you FREE lifetime access to the Reclaim Sobriety On-Demand BootCamp. This exclusive 8-session course is designed to complement your reading, allowing you to dive deeper into the strategies and worksheets at your own pace. Let Ken guide you personally through each exercise, helping you unlock your full potential and solidify your path to lasting sobriety. Don't miss this opportunity to supercharge your recovery journey.

Simply visit reclaimsobriety.com/gift to claim your free access today. Remember, true warriors never stop training – your next level of strength and resilience awaits! go to https://reclaimsobriety.com or scan the QR code.